101 SECRETS TO CAREER SUCCESS

Rashika Fernando

Course Technology PTR

A part of Cengage Learning

COURSE TECHNOLOGY
CENGAGE Learning™

Australia, Brazil, Japan, Korea, Mexico, Singapore, Spain, United Kingdom, United States

COURSE TECHNOLOGY
CENGAGE Learning™

101 Secrets to Career Success
Rashika Fernando

**Publisher and General Manager,
Course Technology PTR:**
Stacy L. Hiquet

**Associate Director of
Marketing:**
Sarah Panella

Manager of Editorial Services:
Heather Talbot

Marketing Manager:
Mark Hughes

Acquisitions Editor:
Mitzi Koontz

Project Editor:
Jenny Davidson

Copy Editor:
Brad Crawford

Interior Layout Tech:
Bill Hartman

Cover Designer:
Mike Tanamachi

Indexer:
Sharon Shock

**Course Technology, a part of
Cengage Learning**
20 Channel Center Street
Boston, MA 02210
USA

Library of Congress Control Number: 2010920334

ISBN-13: 978-1-4354-5722-5

ISBN-10: 1-4354-5722-6

Cengage Learning is a leading provider of customized learning solutions with office locations around the globe, including Singapore, the United Kingdom, Australia, Mexico, Brazil, and Japan. Locate your local office at:
international.cengage.com/region.

Cengage Learning products are represented in Canada by Nelson Education, Ltd.

For your lifelong learning solutions, visit **courseptr.com.**

Visit our corporate Web site at **cengage.com.**

Printed in the United States of America
2 3 4 5 6 7 12 11

This book is dedicated to my lovely wife, Debbie, and our children, Daniella and Shael. They fill my life with love, happiness, and joy and give me purpose. It is through their support that I have been able to accomplish so much in my life.

Acknowledgments

This book was made possible as a result of efforts and contributions of many hardworking and brilliant people. I am grateful for each and every one of them. I would particularly like to acknowledge the following people who made this book possible:

My wife, Debbie, for all the support and suggestions that she provided. She is a living testament to the saying, "Behind every successful man there is a great woman."

Mitzi Koontz is a brilliant acquisitions editor who is open to great ideas. She provided me the opportunity to make this book possible through her dedication and hard work.

Chris Reynolds is a true friend and a great author who introduced me to the world of publishing.

Jenny Davidson is a fervent project editor, whose dedication to this project made this book possible. Brad Crawford is a brilliant copy editor who did an amazing job with wonderful suggestions and great edits that improved the readability of the book. Bill Hartman did an incredible job with the layout and made the book look great. Sharon Shock meticulously indexed the book.

My parents for giving me the right platform and a good background.

Uncle Mahes & Aunty Marie for always being there when we need them and helping us thrive in this wonderful new country that made everything else possible.

My current and past employers and my colleagues through whom I learned so much.

It is a privilege to have such great people supporting me.

About the Author

Rashika Fernando graduated with a Bachelor of Science in Computer Engineering and Business Management from Graceland University in Iowa. After graduating, Rashika went to Sri Lanka to begin his career with IBM Corporation. Within three years, he was managing the largest and the most profitable product line for IBM Sri Lanka as the Product Manager. While working, he completed his Chartered Accounting designation and also Chartered Marketing designation from the UK. Due to the political turmoil in Sri Lanka, Rashika decided to migrate to Canada where he was challenged with beginning his career all over again. Starting as a Coordinator at Canadian Imperial Bank of Commerce, a banking conglomerate in Canada that is one of the top five banks in the country, he quickly rose up within five years to work as a Senior Manager leading the business management team for the Global Finance SBU, which is one of the seven primary business units of the bank.

CONTENTS

Chapter 8
Believe in Yourself 85

Chapter 9
Being Passionate About Your Goals 97

Chapter 10
Identifying and Capitalizing on Opportunities 107

INTRODUCTION

If we distill all the knowledge about success in the world, it boils down to one simple principle—choice. Our choices define us. They determine how we succeed in our careers and in life. We choose to be successful. Nothing happens until we make this choice. Once we decide to be successful, we have taken our first step toward success.

Success means different things to all of us. What does success mean to you? Is it about getting that promotion you always wanted? Or is it seeing your kids grow up well? People go about attaining success in many ways. Success means to achieve the right balance in our lives. When we achieve this balance, we become happy. For all of us, success ultimately means happiness. Happiness is about being content, when what we want in life is there for us. So it is very important for us to define what success means and what happiness looks like.

Some are driven by success, and for some, it means being who they are. Either way, success means the ultimate state of happiness for all of us. It is something that changes from person to person and from time to time for each person. The moment we achieve success, it changes and the bar moves up, because our views change.

Most of us think that work and life are two separate segments, yet they are intermingled in a variety of ways. This is why success should be viewed as a whole rather than two separate facets. This book is about achieving success in your job and also in your life.

Success is a choice that we make. If you boil down all the principles of success to find the one true principle behind everything—it is the principle of choice.

The road to achieving happiness and success, whether material or emotional, requires effort. Putting effort into being successful is a choice that you make. Nobody can make you do anything until you choose. The road to success requires you to make changes to your life and put forth effort. This is based on your choice. You choose to make changes to yourself, and you choose to put effort into making those changes. You choose to move forward despite the fears you might have. Ultimately, you choose to be successful. This book will guide you through that journey, yet you must choose to travel it, to make the necessary changes and move forward.

 Principles of success remain constant over time.

We as humans are constantly driving to achieve things beyond us. Though success is an ever-changing concept, the principles of success remain the same. Regardless of who we are or where we come from, these principles remain constant over time. The principles are the foundation of success. No matter where the road leads you or what your goals are, these principles remain constant.

This book is about principles of success that are fundamental to everyone. They remain constant because long-term success comes from ingrained core principles, principles such as service, hard work, and dedication. They cannot be faked. True mastery of these principles comes from deep understanding rather than a collection of tricks.

The principles of success are not something that I discovered. They have existed since the dawn of time. However, each of us learns them as we move toward our goals in life. Like you, I learned these principles through experience. I wish there were one place I could have gone to learn at least some of them. Imagine the effort and the years saved! There are many self-improvement books about various success principles, yet it was very difficult for me to find one that captured most of the important principles in one place. Nor was it easy for me to learn them through one or two individual experiences. Essentially, principles of success did not come easily to me. That's why I wrote this book—to make your search easier.

Failure should never be underestimated. Sometimes it is far more valuable than success.

Experiences provide us with insights and principles. As we experience life and the outcomes of each situation, we learn what makes us successful and what doesn't. We handle every situation that we encounter based on what we have learned before. This is why, when we go to a job interview, the most important question is about what experience we bring to the job. Though we learn a lot in school, we also learn as much through experience. Most of the soft skills, such as working with people and solving problems, simply cannot be taught in a classroom setting. It comes through being knee-deep in the field, where mistakes and decisions have repercussions! This is why failure is actually far more valuable than winning. Most of the time, the principles that you learn through these experiences and lessons are what determine your success. Experience makes us mature and knowledgeable.

Wouldn't it be nice if there were a way to learn some of the painful lessons of our past without going through those experiences? Some experiences are pleasant and easy to come by, and some are painful and expensive. We build on these lessons and principles. As we go along, they snowball to make us successful and happy.

If you have ever traded on the stock market, you'll know that you're bound to lose money when you start trading. Rarely would you find someone who started making money from the first trade. As you go on, you start making small amounts of money, and then it snowballs. You learn how to manage risk when it comes to money.

Most of us remember at least one instance of how painful it was to deal with a difficult person. As we get older, we become better at it. Similarly, everything in our lives builds on the past. Each generation builds on its predecessors. It is what makes us human.

This book is about a few experiences that taught me some of these lessons. My original intent was to write a collection of essays about my life experiences for my children. I didn't want them to waste time learning through experience what I had already learned. Instead, I wanted them to build on what I had learned. I wanted them to save at least a fraction of the energy that I expended learning these principles that made me successful.

 To be successful, you need to put forth energy and effort.

To learn a success principle, you need to expend energy. We expend energy by thinking, by figuring out, by walking or doing anything (even sitting around). Can you remember a situation when you dealt with a difficult person? Can you remember how tired you were after that incident? You expended energy! You spent so much energy trying to say the right thing or maneuver yourself through the mine fields of things not to say. Once you learned how to deal with difficult people, you didn't expend so much energy the next time because you knew how to deal with similar people again. Now, if you could save half that energy and use it to do something else, imagine what a difference you could make.

I want you to become more successful. With this book, I want you to save at least a fraction of the energy you would have spent picking up the same information over years of day-to-day life. I want to share these principles with you. Collaboration is a great thing, and that is my intent with this collection.

 We succeed through collaboration.

This is not a book of prescriptive lessons, a get-rich-quick scheme, or a lose-weight-in-four-weeks scheme. Success comes through time and living a principled life. You might enjoy modest success by using some isolated techniques, but long-term success and happiness come from a core shift in practicing the correct principles. Success and happiness start with the core, not with techniques.

 There is no point where you can say, "Now I know it all" on your road to success.

These chapters are just a starting point. You probably have additional principles you've developed from your own experiences. There will always be new principles you can learn. The most important message I could hope to convey is that success is a process, not a state. Never stop improving yourself, no matter how old you are. Keep reading and doing research, and combine your own discoveries with what you learn here. I wish you all the best in your journey to success and happiness.

How This Book Is Organized

This book is a collection of articles about different topics on success. Each article provides a number of tips under each topic. Of course, they are not intended to be exhaustive. Whether you are a new graduate or are already in a career, these topics should be invaluable to you. They have certainly served me well. Here's an outline of the chapters.

1. **Your Purpose and Meaning**
   We cannot do anything unless we know why we are doing it. Whether it is your job or a hobby, everything you do in life needs to have a purpose. This is why it is important to start by searching for why you are pursuing the career and life you are. Everything flows from purpose. While goal setting and creating a strategy are wonderful things to do, it makes no sense to work hard if you don't know where you want to go in life. This chapter discusses the importance of, and provides a framework for, discovering a meaning and vision for your career and life.

2. **Success and Happiness**
   We do what we do in order to be happy. This is what success and our careers are all about. This chapter discusses how to keep your eye on happiness and how to build your career to ultimately achieve happiness.

3. **Continuously Improving Yourself**
   We all need to continuously improve ourselves. When we graduate, our learning tends to slow down. Even in our lives, as we age, we stop improving ourselves and try to stick to our old ways. This chapter discusses the importance of improving ourselves and how to do it, not only in terms of skills but also living in and interacting with the world.

4. **Controlling Your Destiny**
   Most people wish that promotions and opportunities would come their way. But successful people are the ones who take control of their destiny and leave very little to chance. Destiny is about making choices and taking action. We become the choices we make and the action we take. This chapter discusses how to control your destiny and positively affect it.

5. **Strategizing Your Career and Life**
   This chapter discusses the importance of strategy in every aspect of career and life, as well as how to apply it. Too often our dreams remain unrealized because we fail to strategize. The chapter also provides a Strategic Planning Framework that can be applied to any goal or dream.

6. **Being Proactive**
   We need to act and be in control in order to get to the outcome we want. In order to do that, we always need to be a step ahead. This chapter describes how to make that happen.

7. **Overcoming Fear**
   One of the biggest inhibitors of success is fear. Fear runs deep within ourselves and dampens our movement toward success. No matter how much we say that we are fearless, we always have some form of fear within us, slowing us down. Though we cannot get rid of fear, we can choose to work around it effectively. This chapter discusses how to summon the courage for that.

8. **Believe in Yourself**
   Though each of us has a purpose and is immensely valuable to this world, we often underestimate this value. In order to succeed, we need to value ourselves accurately, which influences our confidence and perception of the world. We need to believe in ourselves and our abilities. This chapter talks about the importance of self-perception.

9. **Being Passionate About Your Goals**
   Most of us have goals, yet few of us are passionate about them. This is why most goals go unaccomplished. Passion is something you can develop. This chapter discusses the importance of passion for your goals and how to develop it.

10. **Identifying and Capitalizing on Opportunities**
Most people wait for big opportunities to come their way. Because we see only what we want to see, we miss tremendous opportunities as well as smaller opportunities that could lead to bigger ones. Successful people are good at seeing these opportunities. This chapter discusses how to tune in to some of these smaller opportunities and use them to succeed.

11. **Having a Positive Attitude**
It is very easy for us to be negative about the things that go wrong in our lives, yet we rarely realize how adversely this attitude affects our performance and how other people view us. This chapter discusses the importance of maintaining a positive attitude, even in the worst periods of our lives.

12. **Winning in the Long Run**
Victories come in short-term and long-term varieties, and successful people are the ones who keep their eyes on long-term victories. Sometimes we have to give up short-term wins in order to win in the long run. This chapter discusses how to win in the long run.

13. **The Importance of Networking**
We succeed through people. The network of contacts that we have is one of the most important assets for our success. Our networks not only help us gain opportunities but also give back to the world. Without others, success is impossible. This chapter discusses the importance of networking and how to network.

14. **Being Service-Oriented**
Probably you have been to a store that treated you well and also to a store where the personnel were rude. Most of us would rather go to the store where the service was good! Now let's apply this principle to our careers. Management and colleagues are more likely to work well with us if we are service-oriented. Successful people are very service-oriented. This chapter discusses how to be service-oriented and its importance.

15. **Time Management**
    We all have the same 24 hours each day. Successful people are a lot more productive with their time than the average person. Time is one of the most valuable commodities of success. In order to be successful, you need to learn to manage it through prioritization. This chapter provides an overview of the concepts of time management.

16. **Acknowledging Accomplishments**
    We rarely acknowledge our own accomplishments, but doing so can give us a great deal of confidence to move forward. Confidence is crucial for our careers. We tend to remember only our major accomplishments even though we have little accomplishments every day. This chapter discusses how to recognize our accomplishments and build self-confidence.

17. **Living Your Dreams and Making It Happen**
    When we were growing up, we undoubtedly had dreams of becoming successful. Yet once we start working, we can forget those dreams and allow day-to-day reality to overshadow them. Successful people fight for their dreams, and in return their dreams give them tremendous motivation to keep going. This chapter discusses how to start dreaming again or how to hang on to your dreams and make them reality.

CHAPTER 1

YOUR PURPOSE
AND MEANING

Consider two hypothetical organizations: one with a mission and one without a mission. Let me describe the one without the mission first. It's a small business that repairs computers. It has five employees who come in at 9 AM sharp and go home at 5 PM sharp; no one stays late unless overtime is paid. All of them come without any enthusiasm and look like they came to work because they had to come to work. All of them wish they were paid better and at their earliest opportunity will move on to a different job. The only motivation that the owner of this corporation can provide is the promise of a raise.

Now consider an organization with a mission: "To make life better for needy children." This organization also has five employees, but it is a charitable organization, and the employees are tremendously dedicated. Some of them work 14-hour days trying to collect as many donations as possible. Three of them are volunteers working without pay. All of them know their efforts are going toward a cause.

These two organizations illustrate the importance of purpose. Missions give us purpose. Obviously, you would prefer to work for the second organization because it has a purpose. You would look forward to coming to work and would be full of energy when you got there. You wouldn't care what difficulty you had in your work environment. You would still come because you would be driven by the organization's purpose. Your work would have meaning.

Now consider your own purpose. Why do you get out of bed every day? Why do you live and go to work? These are questions that all

1

of us ask at some point in our lives. When you have the answers to these questions, you have purpose and meaning in your life. You are energized.

 Everyone has a purpose. You need only to identify it.

Whether you are a CEO, a banker, or a teacher, your life has a purpose. No matter how insignificant you might think you are, in the overall scheme of things, you still have a purpose. Without you, there would be nobody to fill the gap. The difficulty lies in finding that purpose.

It is important that we all seek this purpose in our lives. Similar to the organizations that I illustrated before, having purpose and meaning gives you a reason to get up in the morning and tackle the day and its challenges. It gives you motivation and energy to do things and make changes to your lives. Most important, having a purpose gives you direction so that you can make good choices.

Do you already know what your purpose should be? If you answered this question quickly, then you are part of a select, clear-thinking crowd. For the rest of us, it takes days, months, years, and sometimes decades to find answers to this age-old question. Even after we do find the answer, it is sometimes not a complete answer.

Questions about our purpose and meaning have been around for centuries. However, there are hardly any generic answers even to this day. This is because the meaning of life is a very complicated and subjective question. It depends on your perception of life, and that's as unique to you as your personality. It is based on your experiences, values, attitude, culture, and many other factors that sometimes even you cannot identify.

However, to have a fruitful life, you need to understand its meaning. This is a basic prerequisite to success. You need to know why you are here and living. Everyone has a purpose, though our individual meanings might differ. Once you know your purpose in life, everything else falls into place. The whole picture starts to take shape.

Wanting to understand your life's purpose is the biggest step forward you can take toward success.

It takes a lot of searching to find the answer that you are seeking. Most of the time, the answer lies right in front of you, even though you never noticed it. All you have to do is "want" to understand it. Then it becomes very obvious to you. Your desire to understand attunes your mind to the search process.

Sometimes humanity gets petty minded about borders, money, and power. You start to understand figures like Gandhi, Christ, and Buddha when you understand the meaning of your life. Everything that they taught essentially boils down to the purpose that we live out in the world. Your purpose is the foundation of your existence. Once you understand this foundation, you start understanding every piece in the puzzle that you call life. It truly is awakening!

 The search for the purpose of your life should start with a search within yourself.

I spent years trying to find out why I was living in this world. I read a number of books searching for the answer, thinking it would be written in some book I hadn't yet read. My search ended up as a deep search within myself for the answer. In this process, I was able to arrive at a framework that assisted me in getting close to the answer. This framework might be a good starting point for anyone searching for their meaning. I'll share it with you.

 Your overall purpose is actually a combination of several components.

It is rare that anyone has just one reason for existence. No matter who you are as a person, you are an integral part of society and the world. In my opinion, your purpose is usually a combination of several components. They generally fall into three groups, which remain constant for most of us. Forming a framework based on these three groups enhances your ability to think through your reasons and ultimately to determine your overall purpose.

Searching for Your Purpose

Why we exist can be boiled down to three foundational reasons:

- To be happy with the life that we have.
- To ensure continuation of life.
- To enhance life.

I think of these three reasons as the Three Pillars of Life.

If you are breathing, you have a life. The first pillar of your life is to enjoy and be happy with this opportunity. As living beings, we also need to ensure our species' survival; thus, we need to contribute toward continuation of life or risk extinction. Furthermore, if we all do nothing to improve the world even in the smallest way we can, we would still be in the Stone Ages. All of us need to contribute to the enhancement of life.

All three pillars need to be fulfilled in order to have a fruitful life. Your purpose is to fulfill these three pillars no matter who you are. You need to take action in each of these three aspects of life in your own way. Let's look at these pillars in detail and see how we ought to craft our purpose for each of these pillars.

Identify What Makes You Happy

To be living in this world is a gift and an opportunity no matter how difficult life becomes. Having the opportunity to experience life is by far the greatest opportunity we all have. We instinctively know this, which is why survival is our primary instinct. Because we have the opportunity of life, we can enjoy all our other opportunities. Whether you believe that it is given to you or not, this opportunity is something that you don't want to miss. Some would even call it a miracle. Whatever label you apply, we must make the most of this opportunity. The only way to do that is to be happy, which is the first pillar of your purpose.

It is important to define what makes you happy.

Happiness is difficult to define. To be happy, you first need to be satisfied. Satisfaction in life means different things to different people. It might mean making a difference in the world, experiencing life to the fullest, or just maintaining your current status. You need to identify what will satisfy you and make you feel happy.

Consider that you've been told that you would not live beyond today. What would you do to make the absolute most of the rest of the day—the rest of your life?

It is important to understand what makes you happy and satisfied. Is it spending time with your family? Is it shopping? Is it living with music? Is it traveling? Whatever it is, it is something that you don't regret spending time on. You need to visualize your final moment and your last breath. If you are spending a lot of time working rather than spending that time with your two-year-old daughter, would you regret this choice in your last moment? Imagine that you've been told that you won't live beyond today. Would that influence your choice to spend time working or with your daughter? The type of choice you make is the ultimate test of happiness. If you are doing something else, then you are not truly happy. This doesn't mean that every individual should be spending their time with a loved one. The time you spend at work could be for the greater good and would make you happier on your dying day. This simple test should reveal your priorities. Only you know the answer.

It is the choices that we make that define us.

This choice is unique to all of us. You need to make the choice that is right for you. Nobody can tell you how to make it. It is a choice of your heart, and it is one of the fundamental choices we make in our lives. The choices that we make define who we are and how we live.

You might also have more than one thing that makes you happy, so don't think that spending time with your family is the only thing that would make you happy.

Decide what makes you happy. Spend time thinking about it. Take time away from work and the rush of everyday life to understand. Sometimes in the rush of things, it is very difficult to get into this level of thought.

Happiness brings a great sense of inner peace. It brings satisfaction to our lives. This inner peace and satisfaction make life worth living. You need to search for this happiness.

Doing What You Love

 Your ultimate career is doing what makes you happy and getting paid to do it.

The ultimate career is doing what makes you happy and earning a living at the same time. Most of us don't fall into this category. More likely, we started on a career track that we stumbled onto when we got out of college, and it might be difficult to change now, as changing means starting all over again.

If what you are doing is not making you happy, then you need to give thought to and strategize about how to change your life. If what you are doing is what makes you happy, try to think about cultivating it more in your life. You can read more about strategy later in this chapter and in Chapter 5, "Strategizing Your Career and Life."

Ensuring the Continuation of Life

 One reason for our existence is being there for each other.

Most of science confirms that we live on a lonely planet (at least with the knowledge that we have today). We humans need to ensure the continuation of our existence. Thus, we need to support the continuation of life. Thousands of years ago, this concept would have meant increasing our numbers. In fact, in today's context, supporting the population growth at the current levels would be contrary to continuation of life. Although this principle has not gone away, it applies to us in the modern day in a very different way. It means to be there for each other. The purpose can be fulfilled in two ways.

1. Continuation of you and your legacy.
2. Helping others to continue life.

Let's look at these two ways separately.

Continuation of You and Your Legacy

All of us want to leave a legacy. We have a finite number of years to live, yet instinctively, we all would like to be remembered.

 One purpose of our existence is to ensure the health and good citizenship of the next generation.

To explain the core concept, forget for a moment about all the permutations of family that exist today, such as single parents and gay marriage. Consider the traditional family. The mother and the father live forever in the genetics and the attitudes that we pass on to our children. Who we are gets passed on in how we bring up our children. We live forever through our children. Bring them up the best way you can. Give them the best you can, and you'll be fulfilling this purpose in life. If you are a parent, you know that this is much easier said than done. However, making the next generation healthy and good citizens is our modern way of supporting the continuation of life.

Bringing up children as good citizens is one way to ensure the continuation of life. However, this isn't the only way to ensure continuation of life. Individual creativity in finding ways to fulfill this aspect of our purpose is also important. For example, there are thousands of children around the world who are orphaned for various reasons. There are many ways to help these children. You can adopt, sponsor a child, or help look after him or her.

Helping Others to Continue Life

 We also need to help this generation continue life.

Ensuring the continuation of life also means helping others continue life. It might be helping a poor family, it might be helping a poor child, or it might be comforting a sick person. In whatever form, we all need to ensure that we assist in the continuation of life by helping one another. We live on a lonely planet.

All of us have problems. You would not be human if you didn't have any problems. They might be financial, physical, or psychological. Whatever their nature, problems are frequently a hindrance to the continuation of life, and helping one another solve contributes toward the continuation of life. It could be as simple as helping your colleague in the next cubicle spell a word correctly or as big as solving world hunger.

The help you lend could be very personal. For instance, your parents might be old and need your help to look after them. You caring for them and doing what you can to make their lives easier is also your contribution toward continuation of life. Whether you conscientiously raise your own children or help others around you in some way—or both—you are fulfilling a core purpose of life. Each of us can do something to help ensure the continuation of life.

Enhancing Life

The third Pillar of Life is to enhance life and add value. We have evolved to be the dominant species on this planet because we keep on enhancing our lives. Each of us has the responsibility to make this world a better place. In essence, you need to add value to the world. You don't need to move mountains to do this, however.

 Enhancing means leaving things at least a little better than we found them.

Enhancing life is all about making this world a better place for you and for others. Everywhere we go and in everything we do, we have the opportunity to improve the people and places around us, to leave them in the same state we found them, or to make them worse. If we left every little thing that we touched in a better state than we originally found it, our world would be a dramatically better place. Essentially, we're adding value to the things in our midst.

Value can come in any form. It might be helping out in an orphanage or just folding an unfolded newspaper on the train that you found and read. Just imagine if all of us understood this concept and followed it. What a great place the world would be! Unfortunately, there are people who destroy life, which is very disheartening. Terrorism, for example, falls in the extreme end of this spectrum. But there are situations when destruction of life happens in very subtle ways. Corruption diverts resources from systems that support life for a country's people. Opposing the people responsible in those situations could be another way of enhancing life.

 Making a difference is not something we always need to do in a big way. Each of us has a small part to play in the big picture.

Each of us can help to enhance life, and we can do it in our own small way. It might be giving a dollar to help someone in need or offering some comforting words to someone facing a difficult challenge. Enhancing life doesn't have to be directed to a stranger. It can be your wife, husband, or child. Surely we're already enhancing the lives of our loved ones, but we all can do a better job at it. Everything we do helps build the big picture. What we do helps build a better world today and tomorrow.

Every grain of sand is needed to build a world. What if all the grains of sand say, "We are going our own way."? Would we have a world? Each of us has a small part to play in the big picture. Enhancing life in our own little way helps in the overall scheme of things in this world.

Not only can all of us do it, but we also can do it anywhere we want. It can be at work. You can leave your workplace in better shape than when you started. You could improve something that you have inherited from someone else. That's just one example. I'm sure you could come up with many creative ways to enhance life for others.

Putting Your Purpose in Action

Mission and strategy are closely connected. You cannot have one without the other. Though it is important to have a purpose, it's only a fancy statement until you do something about it.

Most corporations have visions and purposes, but they rarely do anything with them. Employees come to work and go back home without much motivation. Their mission statements are merely lip service. I once went to a catering shop to pick up food for a family function. On their wall was a plaque with big bold letters at the entrance: "The customer is the most important person ever. The customer is not an interruption of our work." But it only allows customers to pick up food after 11 o'clock. Because my guests were coming for lunch and I wanted to be with them, I asked whether I could pick up my food half an hour earlier, so that I could have enough time for travel and setting up. Despite explaining to them how important it was for me to have it a half-hour earlier, I was told no. Of course, that was the last time I've been there. Examples such as this are numerous in many organizations.

Apply this concept to your personal life; if you have a mission and a purpose, you need to believe in it and execute it. If you have a purpose but don't do anything about it, you might as well not have a purpose. If, after years of soul searching, you learn the true purpose of your life, you need to act on this purpose.

And in order to act on your purpose, you need a strategy. Strategy allows you to connect high-level dreams with actionable plans. Strategy takes this purpose and divides it into actionable plans. It then helps you take these plans and further organize them into actionable projects you can work on daily.

To give you a couple of examples of how to bring your purpose to action, let's look at a charitable organization whose mission is to help hungry children in developing countries. It's a small organization that carries out its mission through specific projects. It has two types of projects:

1. Fund-raising projects to obtain the funds required for the second type of project.

2. Charitable projects that distribute the collected funds to the needy.

The charity might have two fund-raising projects under the first category that aim to generate $2 million through various fund-raising activities in the current year. Each project would have its separate strategy. Furthermore, the organization might have two charitable projects, one in Sri Lanka and another in Uganda. Each project would have its strategy for assisting children in each country.

Similarly, a man who has a mission to aid others through his knowledge might execute that vision the following ways:

1. Running day-to-day life: You cannot execute your purpose if you don't have a means to live. This class of projects would ensure his survival. Sub-projects might include:

   ■ Getting promoted to a manager.

   ■ Buying a decent house to live in.

   Though these projects are not directly related to his primary mission, they support the primary mission. Without these support projects, he cannot execute the primary mission.

2. Adding value to others' lives: Now that he has a platform to sustain him through the first class of projects, he can execute the following projects to achieve his mission.

   ■ Write a book to share his knowledge.

   ■ Work part time helping at an old-age home.

Similarly, when it comes to executing your primary purpose, your strategy might have two or more classes of strategic priorities:

1. Primary strategy: This strategy is directly related to your primary purpose. The strategy would have specific deliverables that would impact forward movement against your purpose. There may be several projects or strategies under this category.

2. Support strategy: In order to support your primary strategy, you need to sustain yourself. Projects under this category would ensure that your sustenance is maintained. Though they don't directly impact your purpose, without these projects you would not be able to work on your mission and purpose.

Thus, you need to have a strategy to support your mission. Strategy takes your purpose and mission to the next level. The relationship could be depicted with the diagram shown below.

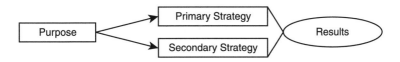

You get a fulfilling feeling when you actually do progress on these projects and strategies. Because they are connected with your purpose, no matter how difficult these projects are and how much work is involved, you get a sense of accomplishment when you work on them. Chapter 5 discusses in detail how to take your purpose to the level that we can act on it. Most of us procrastinate on the most important things in life because we have difficulty figuring out the action plan to implement them or the next action to take. By doing a strategic-planning exercise, you can figure out the details behind your purpose and act on them.

 Creativity is an important factor in trying to enhance life. All of us are born with it.

Creativity is also an important factor in trying to enhance life. All of us are born with the ability to create, and there are many ways in which we could enhance life. We just have to think of them. Making that effort is also part of our responsibility to enhance life.

A lot of people give money to charities to help others. This is certainly one way of enhancing life, but you don't need money to help others. You could sit with a lonely senior and spend time with him. Another creative example comes from the movie *Pay It Forward*. In it, a small boy invents the concept of paying it forward: He does something good for three people that he comes across. In return, he asks those three people to do something good for three other people. It is like a chain letter, but it is a chain letter of good deeds. It has an exponential effect.

We need to make things better for others. We do it not to gain benefit but purely to enhance the life of others. The return that we get is that we feel accomplished.

Conclusion

We all live for a purpose. The purpose we each live for is unique to us and defines us. However, the most difficult challenge is understanding this purpose. We can think about it for years and years and yet not find the answer that we are seeking. If you really look at life, the three aspects to our purpose can help us understand things better. As stated earlier, they are:

- To be happy with the life that we have.
- To ensure continuation of life.
- To enhance life.

CHAPTER 2

SUCCESS AND HAPPINESS

W e all strive for happiness. Most everything that we do on a daily basis we do to achieve a state of happiness. Knowingly or unknowingly, it is what drives and motivates us. Whether it is in our careers, studies, or family lives, happiness is what we ultimately want to achieve.

Success and happiness are related but not the same thing.

Success and happiness are often thought of as the same thing. There is sometimes the misconception that success will lead to happiness. Though the two principles are related, they are not the same. Most of the time, success will lead to happiness, but not all the time.

In our journey toward success, we must never forget the purpose of the journey. This is why knowing the meaning and purpose of your life is important. Everything that we do should be aligned with our purpose. Being happy is the ultimate success that we are trying to achieve.

A lot of people, many of them smart, well-educated individuals, do not fully understand this concept, though they think they do. Happiness is about being content while pushing yourself to be your best.

When trying to find a balance between happiness and success, you will discover that there are three states:

1. Being truly happy and being content.
2. Being successful at the cost of happiness.
3. Being happy at the cost of success.

You can draw these three states on a spectrum as shown below:

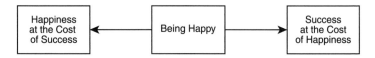

Being happy and content is the midpoint on this spectrum. This life is a privilege, so you don't want to live without achieving your potential. At the same time, you don't want your life to fall apart. True success is the middle path, because you would be both successful and happy in this state.

Happiness is not about taking things easy. Yes, it is very easy to be lazy by saying we want to be happy. We might be happy, but we would be wasting our lives by not reaching our potential. To reach your potential means to push yourself to the limit to achieve your dreams. It will be stressful. Stress is a fact of life. You will have difficulty and rough spots in life. Life is painful, and success can be extremely painful. Being happy does not mean that we avoid this pain. Of course, being lazy would bring certain benefits to you, but it is a superficial form of happiness. True happiness comes from success in all aspects of your life.

A very intelligent colleague of mine was recently talking to me about her future. She is fully capable of reaching much higher in her career than where she is now. When I recommended that she should attempt reaching higher, she mentioned that reaching higher would mean additional stress and additional work hours, even though in reality it didn't mean compromising her family life by working a few extra hours. I felt that this was just a self-fulfilling excuse given to run away from the pain of reaching higher. Though she was telling me that her personal life might get compromised, I think she knew that pushing herself a bit more wouldn't make a difference. Every time I meet her, she asks me how difficult it is to be a few levels higher in my career than she is so that she can justify to herself why she is not pushing herself to the limit.

Similar to my colleague, there are many who justify themselves and stay within their comfort zones by saying that working hard will be stressful and unhappy. You need to push yourself to achieve great things. Achieving great things requires hard work. You cannot sit on your couch and expect great things to happen.

The other extreme is that you would work so hard that other areas of your life are falling apart. I have met a few colleagues who have made this mistake. Their families are not happy because they work too much and pay too little attention to what matters the most. For them, achieving great positions in their careers is worth any cost.

To be truly happy and successful, you should not fall into either of these extremes. Success should come from holding your life together while pushing yourself to excel. The middle path is not easy.

The purpose of the journey should not be forgotten. At the end of the day, I'm sure all these people will wonder where their years have gone. Passing time cannot be regained. We all have a finite number of years in our lives, even if we like to think otherwise.

Success should be viewed in a holistic way where you succeed in all aspects of life, instead of a few. For example, working hard and ignoring your health will lead to bad repercussions later in life and cause unhappiness, even though you would have great resources as a result of your success.

 Real success is achieving in all aspects of your life and enjoying yourself along the way.

Happiness is the end, while success is only a means to an end. Success should not be viewed as having the top job or the biggest house. It is not about going to the top at any cost. When you succeed in only a few aspects of your life, you create tremendous vacuums in other areas of your life. You need to avoid vacuums and pursue balance. Real success is achieving in all aspects of your life and enjoying yourself along the way. This is what I call happiness.

We all strive to achieve what makes us happy. For example, you might be striving to achieve a top job that will pay you a million dollars a year. The reason that you are trying to achieve that job could be that you will have plenty of money to enjoy your time with your family and lead a comfortable life. But in the process, if you ignore the balance, you might actually end up alienating your family. When you do attain the job you desired after years of hard work, you might realize that your kids have grown up and you have lost the family you always wanted to enjoy. So what's the point of working so hard to achieve that top job? You wasted the most important years achieving nothing.

You need to balance your success and do the things you love.

Happiness is when you balance your success and do things that you love to do. Finding what you love and creating a balance is challenging. For most of us, the journey starts when we are growing up. We get pushed into different career streams. At that time, there is little information about how it is going to be when actually we get into a career. However, in our immature states of mind, we are compelled to make choices, and we spend a lot of time preparing for the careers we chose. It might be several years, after college and perhaps graduate school and postgraduate studies, before we realize whether our choices were good or bad. For too many of us, it ends up being the wrong choice, because we have changed as people, matured and discovered new things. Or we realize it wasn't something we wanted to do in the first place. By this time it might be too late to go back, or we just don't want to start all over again. We might have children or other responsibilities that prevent us from returning to school, so we continue down the same unsatisfying path. Was it worth it?

Most of this problem exists because we equate success with money. We gravitate to choices that have the most money attached to them and not the ones that we love doing. We work very hard day to day to please our bosses, keep our children healthy, and manage our lives. At the end of the day we're exhausted and haven't achieved anything. What did we do all day? Where did we spend all our time? We just ran in the same place.

Understand the root causes of your happiness.

To solve this problem, or avoid it in the first place, you need to understand the root causes of your own happiness. What are you really trying to achieve with all the effort that you are putting into becoming successful? You need to really look hard at what you want in your life, irrespective of the effort. This is really important because you might be striving very hard to achieve an interim goal that would get you only halfway to happiness.

Understanding root causes means understanding what makes you happy deep down inside. Finding the causes of happiness for each of us is different, and how we go about it is different. We all think differently. Understanding causes comes from having a deep understanding of yourself and what makes you happy. Nobody can dictate to you what will make you happy.

Searching for this cause means understanding your purpose, and it relates to what I discussed in Chapter 1 about the meaning of life. All our efforts should be connected to our purpose, which is what drives us. When we don't make a connection to our purpose, we feel depleted and used.

As long as our hard work is connected to our purpose, it does not feel like hard work. For example, you might be writing a book about something you love and driving toward a deadline to get all your material published. If it is connected to your purpose, no matter how many hours you put into writing, even without a break, it would not make you feel depleted; you would feel fulfilled. Compare this to someone who is working for a paycheck and doing a couple of hours of e-mails. That person would be exhausted. Work is not work as long as you are enjoying it!

You need to strategize to achieve this state of happiness. You need to strategize on how you are going to juggle your existing lifestyle and achieve your goals. Strategy is one of the most important tools to help us lead a very successful life. We grow up instinctively knowing how to strategize, but we rarely cultivate this skill. To achieve your happiness, you need to have a strategy. Once you know where you are heading, then getting there can be achieved through your strategy.

At one time I was going after the top job because I wanted to be somebody. Reason: I wanted to make a difference in the world. Over time, however, I realized that I didn't have to have the top job to make a difference for people. It was only one alternative. To get to the top job, I might have wasted a lot of time and effort. Creativity was the only factor I was lacking finding the answer. I was looking for happiness in the wrong place. Sometimes the most obvious place to find happiness is not the best place to look.

 Look deep in your heart to seek what you are trying to achieve by being successful.

In the chapter about your purpose and meaning, I've talked about what your purpose in life is and how to identify it. To understand what makes you happy, you need to understand your purpose. It stems from what you feel is the reason for your existence. In order to understand this, you need to forget about what society would say about what you want. Look deep in your heart at what you are trying to achieve. To understand your true motivations, your spouse, partner, or friends can really help put things in perspective. Whatever approach you take, try to understand the real drivers of your happiness and what you are trying to achieve.

Ideally, your definition of success should be the same as your purpose. Unfortunately, we tend to gravitate toward money and material possessions, because they can be seductive and addictive. You need to have two streams in your life—one to satisfy the world and the other to satisfy yourself. This will bring a sense of great achievement. Not only will you be able to enjoy the world but you also will be very happy as well.

 Creativity is an important factor in achieving happiness.

You also need to cultivate your creativity to achieve happiness. There are thousands of ways to achieve your goals. Sometimes you might need to cultivate a parallel stream of activities to achieve your happiness. In a lot of chapters, I'll talk about creativity. Creativity is very important when it comes to your success and happiness. I cannot stress enough the importance of creativity in every aspect of your life and career. Like my daughter's children's movie says, "Think, think, think." We all need to think and let our minds run free.

To be happy and successful, you must have ideas. You need to trust your ideas and have faith in them. Once you have faith in yourself and your ideas, your mind will start generating great ideas. Your mind seems to operate on your command and how you treat it. If you treat it well, it will provide the creativity you need to generate wonderful ideas.

You have to let your mind run free without judgment and give yourself time to think. Sometimes we are so busy that we don't give ourselves time to think. I have met so many people who are running around trying to find jobs, doing children's chores, fixing houses, and trying to fix their families, but few actually stop and think. Giving yourself time to think is really important. Working hard without being creative is like trying to cut a tree without sharpening the axe. You'd be hitting the tree very hard but making very little progress.

Conclusion

Try to define success as things that make you happy. You will feel much more fulfilled than a lot of people. And once you define success, you will then be able to strategize on how you can get it.

Chapter 3

Continuously Improving Yourself

Continuous self-improvement is one of the foundations of success. If you are to succeed in your career and your life, you need to make this one of your primary beliefs. Success is about becoming a better person. Humanity has progressed, and we have become the dominant species because we can improve ourselves.

Different people have different attitudes toward improving themselves, but without the desire to do it, no one makes very much progress no matter what resources they might otherwise have. People who have the desire to be better will improve themselves even with few resources. The world might not believe in them, but the desire they have enables them to believe in themselves and catapult beyond the norms of the world. Great leaders who came out of nowhere all got there because they had the desire to better themselves and make a difference.

It is in our nature to be better, yet too few of us actually cultivate this desire. To be successful, you need to tap into this ability. No doubt the reason you're reading this book is because you want to be a better person—you are one of the few who are cultivating this trait. It is this gift that differentiates us from the rest of the living beings in the universe. We can always strive to be better than what we are, something I'm deeply grateful for. It's amazing that we have this ability, and it is all within our control.

This chapter walks you through the basics of self-improvement and making self-improvement work for you, regardless of the goals you have. The principle of self-improvement is within all of us.

What Is Self-Improvement?

Self-improvement is a directed effort beyond our natural maturing process.

Self-improvement is about actively changing yourself for the better. All of us mature naturally over time, but self-improvement is a directed effort rather than a natural maturing process. We are not born perfect. We can all improve ourselves for the better.

There will be a gap between what we are today and where we need to be based on our mission. In order to close this gap, we need to change our habits and develop our skills—to improve ourselves. In order to do that, we must identify where we can improve, set goals, and execute a strategy to achieve them—all of the principles in this book are interconnected.

In order to be successful, you need to change, which means improving yourself.

Not everybody can be successful. In order to be successful, you need to change and improve yourself. If you don't improve yourself, you will be stuck in the same comfort zone. Successful people are the ones who constantly improve themselves. Every day the world is constantly improving. If you are to be successful, you need to exceed the pace of the world around you and rise above the rest. In order to do that, you need a self-improvement strategy.

To improve ourselves, we need to be courageous.

We all have different reasons not to change and improve ourselves. These are all self-fulfilling prophesies. Whether it is a reason like, "Oh, it's not for me ..." or "I can't do it because of my commitments ... ," it will only keep you from your best. Fear of the unknown is the common reason behind most of the excuses we give against self-improvement and change. In order for us to improve ourselves and change, we need to move forward with courage. Being courageous does not mean that we move forward without fear; it means moving forward despite our fears. It is a choice that we make when we decide to be courageous. We all have fear. The courageous make a choice to go forward and risk it all despite their fear.

Self-improvement efforts need to have at least four elements.

A personal self-improvement strategy should have the following components:

1. Identify the areas you need to improve.
2. Have goals and targets for improvement.
3. Have an approach and strategy for improvement.
4. Have a way to measure your progress.

This strategy might not be an explicitly written strategy, but most of our active self-improvement needs should have these elements.

You will notice that these are the same components of strategy when you read the strategy chapter. Your success relies on your self-improvement strategy. Because of this, let's look at self-improvement strategy in detail:

1. **Identify the areas you need to improve:** The areas of improvement are the gap between where you want to be and your current self. In order for you to be successful, you need to take responsibility for your own development and identify these gaps: what you have to do in order to go on to the next level or even to secure your current position, such as your job. We all have our egos, and we are stubborn to some extent no matter who we are. This is actually one of the biggest obstacles to our success. It is we who keep us away from our best. When it comes to identifying the need to improve, we have to humble ourselves. I'm not saying that you have to give up your self-worth to be successful, even though some give this

excuse for not working hard. At least to ourselves, we have to be truthful and admit the weaknesses that we have. We are all intelligent people. We know the areas that we have to work on. We have to look hard at ourselves and understand what we truly can improve on. This is what I mean by identifying the areas of improvement. Real success comes by first succeeding within. You need to have your principles correct. In order to have your principles correct, you need to understand how you see the world. We all see the world through our own lenses. We have to have the correct lens to see ourselves correctly. Then we can identify areas that we can improve.

2. **Have goals and targets for improvement:** Once we identify the areas that we need to improve, we need to have goals in place. Otherwise, we would not know how we have improved. I know it can be difficult to think of goals for certain things in life. For example, if you are trying to improve your outlook on your interactions with friends, there is nothing you can measure. But, at least after two years, you could use your common sense to gauge whether you have improved on this aspect of your life, such as having three close friends rather than none. Things such as weight loss and your income can be quantitatively measured and assessed. The primary idea behind having goals is to be able to visualize where you want to be. You have to be able to define what success looks like. It is vital that you are able to see and feel what success looks like even before you make any effort. This is what I mean by having goals and targets in place for improvement.

3. **Have an approach and strategy for improvement:** We need to have an approach and a strategy for everything we do, a breakdown of the work effort involved in achieving the goal. Creativity is an important skill that you need to develop when you come up with your approach. In Chapter 5, I delve into the details of the approach. Of course, once you have an approach, then you need to put effort into acting on your strategy.

4. **Have a way to measure your progress:** As important as
   having a strategy and goals is, it is just as important to measure your improvement. From time to time, you must ask, "Is
   this working for me?" You might have quantitative measure-
   ments for certain self-improvement strategies, such as the
   amount of savings you have in the bank, but there are other
   strategies you cannot quantify. In such situations, you need to
   take an honest look at yourself and ask hard questions on the
   effectiveness of your strategy. If your strategy is not working,
   then you need to make changes.

If you are to be successful, you need to catapult yourself ahead of others.

We as humans are born to evolve. No matter what level of success
we achieve, we always want to go to the next level. It does not matter who we are or what we do. We always want to achieve something higher. Self-improvement stems from this basic human need,
the need to be something greater than what we are. It is as basic as
our need for water and air. It is what moves us forward as a species.
However, in a competitive situation, we need to catapult ourselves
ahead of others. We need to be cognizant of the fact that our competition is constantly improving. Yet we need to move ahead while
maintaining the balance.

Our mistakes form the basis of our learning and improvement.

Self-improvement also stems from the fact that as humans, we learn
from our mistakes. I am a better and a stronger person today because
of the mistakes that I have made in the past, however big or small
they were. When we make mistakes, we discover how to avoid making the same mistake again. In order for us to avoid a mistake, we
need to improve. This process of improvement doesn't stop at any
point in time or at a certain age. We improve ourselves all the time.
This is one process that continues until we die, just like breathing and
eating.

Since this is a natural process that we are born with, we certainly have the need to excel at this process. This process is a foundation of our success. Thus, we need to learn to improve ourselves. It is something that is learned and acquired rather than inherited.

Genetics and Self-Improvement

Though we don't realize it, there is hardly anything that we inherit in our personalities and abilities. Most of our personalities are learned at some point in our lives. I am a firm believer that who we are depends on what we learn and on our choices and our experiences.

Changing yourself is all about valuing and loving yourself.

Think about this: If we as humans inherited most of the traits, the human race would not have progressed as far as we've come today. It is because we have a choice between what our ancestors did and what we do that each generation does better than the previous. It is our innate ability to learn and change ourselves that has enabled our species to excel beyond all living things in this universe. It is a choice that we have to make. Changing yourself is all about loving yourself. We love ourselves when we choose to rise above our own laziness and make the effort. We all have the ability to change ourselves, but few of us actually choose to do it. The fact that we can learn means that we can change ourselves in everything that we do. Many of our traits are learned; therefore, our traits can be unlearned and relearned.

As humans, we are able to break away from what our ancestors did and do things better and differently. When we are born, we are born with certain skills. These skills enable us to survive in our early years. However, as we grow up, we don't need these initial skills. Yet some of us hold on to them. Successful people go through the pain of giving up these habits to learn new ones. We are equipped with the ability to change these skills and learn new ones. This is how we progress in life and as a society.

Our willingness to change and improve ourselves is a foundation of our success.

One of the most important factors of self-improvement is our willingness to change. If we are willing to change, we can do almost anything. There are a lot of things in life that we might like to be different. However, willingness is about wanting to be different or to change. It is a deep motivation to achieve your goal. We will talk about it more later on.

Let's say you wanted to lose weight. Have you ever wondered why people give up their new diet or exercise schedules so quickly? It is because their motivation to change is driven more by what they like than what they want. If the willingness is there, they'll be motivated to lose weight regardless of the effort involved.

Improving Yourself

 Self-improvement always requires time and effort.

You need to invest in the change that you need. This investment is mainly about time and effort. Most important, it is a choice that you make. If you are willing to put effort into improving yourself, very soon you will see results.

To invest time and effort, you need to be committed. This is a commitment that you make to yourself. It is very important not to break this commitment because breaking a commitment with yourself would result in losing your self-worth and self-integrity, so be sure when you are committing yourself.

Making a commitment is great, but it is not going to take you to your goal. You first need a strategy and a plan.

Like vs. Want—The Difference

Once you have decided to invest time and effort, you need a plan—a goal and a strategy.

One of the most important factors is our willingness to change. There are many factors that motivate people. However, most of our motivations are driven by something you love or something you fear. It is this motivation that drives the need to change. When there is a need, the change is permanent, while if you change because you like something, your change is usually temporary. We tend to revert back to our old ways quickly.

When thinking of improving yourself, distinguish between what you like and what you really want to change. If it is something you like to change, it is important to first convert your "like" to a "want." You need to identify what is driving your need to change. At the same time, you need to identify the consequences of not changing.

If the consequences of not changing yourself are acceptable to you, you will not go far with your self-improvement. It is because your motivation is not strong enough to carry you through all the phases of the self-improvement process. You would start the change actions in the short term, but in the long term, you would find it difficult to maintain your action plan.

Self-improvement requires energy and effort. The energy will come from how motivated you are about your choices. This motivation is very important. Initially, when you start a self-improvement process, you will have this energy, because you are excited that you are going to change something. However, when the excitement dies off, you need to have a deep motivation to exert continuous energy in your self-improvement project.

Three Stages of Self-Improvement

There are three stages of self-improvement. Most of your self-improvement projects will fall into this framework.

1. **Short term:** The first few days of your self-improvement. During this stage, you will have a lot of enthusiasm about making a change. The first few actions in the project will be easily done. It is important that you understand that your enthusiasm and your motivation will be generally short lived. We are like matches; most of the time, when we start something, we are excited and energetic. After a while, our energy drops and the work involved becomes mundane. Having worked for a large technology division, I have seen this day in and day out. All the work was primarily based on projects. When new projects came down the pipeline, everybody in the division was excited. Everybody wanted to get into the next hot project. However, as time went by, the excitement started to wear off. Some of the large multiyear projects actually became burdens for a lot of the management. They couldn't wait for the very project that they were so excited about at the start to end. How quickly the excitement wears off will differ based on what you are trying to improve.

2. **Mid term:** This is the most difficult phase of any self-improvement project. In this stage, your initial enthusiasm has dried up, and your resistance to change kicks in. You require a lot of energy in this phase to make the change effective. Your old habits will take your life back again if you are not watchful. Most of our self-improvement projects die off in the mid term without our ever reaching the goal. It is important to remind ourselves of the motivations behind our improvement process. One way to sustain the forward momentum is to break down your efforts into mini-projects. This way you can maintain the initial excitement over achieving an immediate goal. We'll look at how to do this later in the chapter. As with the short-term phase, the duration of this phase will differ for each person and each goal.

3. **Long term:** This is the easiest phase. If you were successful in the short term and mid term, you will have instilled in yourself the change you made as a habit. Your new habit is actually a new way of life. The only thing you have to watch out for is not to go back to your old ways. Very few of our projects reach this phase because it is so difficult to cross the mid-term chasm. Your strategy needs to account for this difficulty.

The energy that you put into this change is your investment. It is the effort that you put in to obtain a better result in the future.

Putting It All to Work

So how do you put all of this to work? It is much easier than you think. It requires a good plan that is well-thought-through, and it boils down to your strategy. This plan needs to be practical and workable.

Any change requires careful thought and planning.

Before you do anything, you need to decide the change that you want. You need to envision it and define it. Without defining the end result, it would be very difficult for you to strategize. In order to define what you want, you first need to identify what your current position is and then set a goal to improve the current situation. Let's look at an example.

Let's say I want to lose weight. I am overweight and unhappy about it. I don't like the way society sees me, and I want to improve my appearance. My ideal state is that of a normal person. In order to do this, I need to lose 60 pounds. That is my goal. (I didn't write down my goal in this case, since it was so obvious—I was always carrying it with me. Some of your goals might work that way too.)

It would be great if you write down your current situation and your goals. However, sometimes, there are things that are so obvious, you don't need to write it down.

What motivates me to lose weight? If I continue to be overweight, I will have serious health issues in the future. I could lose years from my lifetime and would spend the latter part of it suffering from health complications. I can't accept these consequences.

The next step is to strategize on how to achieve this goal. I talk about how to strategize in Chapter 5, so I will not go into detail here. However, strategy is all about having a high-level approach to achieving this goal. In this situation, how do I go about losing 60 pounds? It seems to be an awful lot of effort to lose 60 pounds. My strategy would be as follows:

- **Phase I:** Focus on losing 10 pounds first. Even this can be broken down further as 10 pounds could be quite difficult in practical terms. So, I'll aim to lose 2 pounds in the first week and 2 pounds in each subsequent week going forward.

- **Phase II:** Lose 20 pounds next. I won't think about "how" until I come close to finishing Phase I.

- **Phase III:** Lose another 20 pounds. By now, my new lifestyle will have become a habit.

- **Phase IV:** Lose the remaining 10 pounds and think about exiting the weight loss phase and entering the maintenance phase. I will focus on exercise mainly but supplement that method with a healthy diet.

This is a simple example of a strategy. Once you decide on the strategy, then you can approach the tactics. For example, how often should I work out? What exercises should I do? How many miles should I run? These are the details of the strategy.

It is sometimes difficult to distinguish between strategy and tactics. Strategy and tactics merge well with each other. If you are working on a large project, tactics of one strategy become the strategy in the next layer. However, it is important to understand the broad differences.

Once you strategize and decide on the tactics, you have to be committed to your strategy. As mentioned earlier, your commitment needs to be primarily in the medium term. You have to be committed to achieving your strategic goal. Be willing to change your plans, but refuse to change your goals.

If your goal is something you would like to achieve rather than something you want, you need to find the motivation to change it to a want. If not, once the initial steam wears off in your strategy, you will likely lose interest. You need to believe in what you want to achieve. That is the discipline that will see you to your goal.

At the same time, monitor your self-improvement efforts. As you do, you'll need to make changes to your original plan based on your observations. If some of your tactics or some part of your strategy isn't working, you need to change the plan. The idea is to achieve the final goal, not to finish the plan. Sometimes we lose sight of the goal once we have a plan. Your plan and your strategy are just a means to an end.

Conclusion

We all need to improve ourselves. We all have the innate ability to unlearn traits and relearn new traits. As humans, this is how we have evolved. In order to be successful, we have to tap in to our ability to improve ourselves and harness this ability.

It is in our nature to improve ourselves, but most of our self-improvement needs to be done consciously. We have to direct our effort toward improving ourselves to meet our goals. Sometimes, this means being courageous. When we venture in self-improvement, we are going to the unknown. We are trying to learn something new. This requires us to put aside our fears about the unknown and be courageous.

Any self-improvement effort has at least four elements. In this chapter, we discussed these elements. It is important that we think of any directed self-improvement effort in terms of these four elements. Moreover, once we start our self-improvement initiatives, it goes through at least three stages. Of these three, we discussed that the second stage is what requires our most effort.

Finally, in order to make self-improvement work for us, we need to have a strategy and a plan. It is very important that we strategize our self-improvement efforts.

CHAPTER 4

CONTROLLING
YOUR DESTINY

O ur choices define us. How we choose determines our destiny. You are the driver of your life. Everything that you have done, are doing right now, and will do in the future impacts your destiny. Destiny is a product of the choices that we make during our lives and the actions that we take. Destiny is not a gift that was given or written in the stars.

There are a range of views about destiny. Various cultures believe that destiny is written on your palm or in the stars when you are born. However, if you look at your past, you will realize that who you are today is a result of the choices you made and the actions you took. You could have done it differently, even in situations where you think that you didn't have a choice. Controlling your destiny is a matter of strategizing and taking action.

Choosing Your Destiny

 To be successful, you need to learn to choose and make decisions.

On your road to success, it is very important to learn how to choose. Choosing requires you to be brave and fly in the face of fear, because choosing is taking risk and taking responsibility for your choices. This is not a skill that only successful and rich people have; it is a skill that we all learn. What differentiates the high performer from the rest is that he or she makes a choice when the rest of the world would be stuck in the middle. It might not be the correct choice, but it is still a choice.

Choice requires us to side with one opportunity. All opportunities have their merits, but we can select only one at a time. What most of us have difficulty doing is selecting just one. Most of us are attracted to all the opportunities in front of us, and we hesitate to make that choice.

Let's take a typical example of weight loss. Most of us would like to lose a few pounds yet have a difficult time doing so. If you really look at the reasons, it is a problem of choice. We want to enjoy the pleasure of food that we eat, but we are also attracted to appearing better physically. This is why most of our weight-loss efforts fail—we have not made a choice to give up one of the opportunities. We are stuck in the middle. When people get health complications, they have no problem getting on a rigorous diet and exercise schedule that they had difficulty even contemplating before. Why? The choice is no longer available.

Choosing means giving up one thing (including all its merits!) for another.

You need to learn to give up some opportunities in return for better opportunities. Life is all about making choices and compromises. I knew several very intelligent colleagues in my career who have made the mistake of not choosing. They had wonderful job opportunities that came their way, but because they didn't want to sacrifice one choice for another, their careers haven't advanced. On your road to success, you can't be greedy.

It is risky to choose. Nevertheless, you still need to choose or risk being stuck in the middle.

Making a choice is difficult because of the risk involved. I guarantee you that some of the choices you make will result in mistakes. You cannot run away from making mistakes. Making tough choices in life is risky, but you still need to make them. If you don't, it will be very difficult to progress in your career and in life. When you make mistakes, forgive yourself, learn from them, and move on.

A few years ago, I received a large sum of money. I had many opportunities in front of me:

1. Invest this money in the stock market for a short-term return.
2. Use it for postgraduate work, which will give me a return later.
3. Invest in my retirement for a long-term return.

All these options were attractive, but I chose the first option. I had my reasons. In the midst of a stock market meltdown, I lost most of this money. It was a mistake that became evident only after it had happened. Instead of worrying about the mistake I made, I moved on. I learned a lot from that experience. The lessons that I learned were very expensive but well worth it. The most important lesson I learned was that even after making a mistake, I would still be okay, and the same would apply to most of your choices. You might make mistakes with your choices, but in the end you will still be okay. The experience gave me confidence to move forward.

In your career and life, it is important that you make a choice and work on that choice.

Destiny Is Within Your Reach

Not only is it important to choose, but once you choose, you also need to take action.

Destiny is the outcome of all the decisions and actions we take. The word "destiny" has the same root as "destination." Your destiny could be anything from achieving a single dream to being somebody that you want to be. Destiny is the ultimate destination. It is the outcome of the sequence of events in your life. Nobody knows whether your destiny is written in the stars or some secret book. However, based on my experience, it is something that is completely within our control.

Your journey to your final destination is filled with moments when you need to make decisions and take action. These are what I call junctions. At each junction, you can take action to change the course or stay on the current path. The moment you take action, you shift toward your desired destination. But that desired destination might not be where your current path is leading. These junctions are opportunities; pay close attention to them. It is very easy to miss a junction. We miss so many junctions every day in our lives, without recognizing them for what they are.

Choices, ideas, and desires are the first step toward your destiny. They give us direction and guidance. Without knowing where to go and what direction to take, you cannot start. However, without action, you would be sitting in the same place. Many people have great ideas, but very few actually take the steps to implement their ideas. To be successful, you need to take action and implement your ideas.

 You need to know the next thing to do to implement your ideas.

A journey to the moon starts with a first step out of your house. You have to take action to implement that next thing that will move you one step closer to your destination.

Telling you to take action is easy, but taking action in reality is difficult. Let's discuss what I mean by taking action. Taking action means being committed to doing something about your destiny. We either can live in a dream or take action to make that dream come true. The choice is yours. When we make a commitment to ourselves, we're making a promise. Being committed and making promises to ourselves means exerting effort toward our destiny. As simple as it sounds, making an effort is difficult. It requires us to think and go out of our way. However, it is a choice that we make. We have to consciously make a choice to put forth effort and make a commitment.

Once you make a commitment, you need to make your dreams happen. You need to make sacrifices and give of yourself completely to achieve your destiny. This is what commitment requires us to do. A lot of us are not willing to do this, which is why our destinies remain only dreams.

To achieve your destiny, you need to define what it looks like and have a strategy to achieve it. The next chapter discusses in detail how you can approach your goals. The first step toward achieving your destiny is to give detailed thought to your goals and how to achieve them. Most of the time, we hesitate to give thought to anything, feeling that our ideas might not be adequate. As a result, we sit in limbo, and destiny becomes only a dream. You need to break down your goals and have a detailed idea on how to achieve them.

Fear and laziness are the fundamental reasons we fail to take action.

Of course, many reasons keep us from taking action toward our destinies. I could say that I don't have time, or I don't have the resources or the skills. But, if you really boil down these reasons, there are essentially two reasons: fear and laziness.

There are many forms of fear. Fear of being inadequate, fear of the unknown, fear of change, fear of confrontation. The list goes on. Whatever form it is, it is the same feeling, and this feeling will stop you dead in your tracks. We often don't admit that we are fearful. Though subconsciously we are fearful, we give other reasons for lack of action. Being truthful to yourself and searching deep within yourself will reveal that most of the reasons that you give for not taking action have the same common denominator. All of us have fear, but you can choose to move forward despite the fears that you have. You have to overcome your fears for you to be successful.

Laziness is the other factor that keeps us from success. It is human nature to be lazy. We all need rest, and we all need to be lazy. Making an effort to be successful is against the concept of laziness. Yet we need to overcome the laziness in us to be successful and to achieve our goals. Again, it is a choice. Similar to fear, most of us don't want to admit that we are lazy. But, once you identify what is keeping you away from your success, you can make a choice to overcome it.

Don't give yourself excuses. Excuses might make you feel good, but they will never give you what you want.

When you make excuses, you give yourself reasons not to take the road less traveled. Excuses provide a good feeling about the wrong choices that we make. Every time you give yourself an excuse, you subconsciously reinforce taking the easy way out. My advice is, rather than giving an excuse, learn to manage the situation, take responsibility, make a choice, and take action. Don't give yourself excuses for not taking action. Discipline yourself, and do it despite what you feel.

Let's say the only reason you can't complete your master's degree is that you don't have time—you're a single parent with three children and a tough job. You could learn time management as the first step. By learning to manage your time, you could get creative. For example, you could find a babysitter to look after your children for two hours a day. Prioritize what you have to do.

Myths About Destiny

 Despite the myths about destiny, it is within your control.

There are many myths about destiny. People can get very superstitious about it. Some believe that their destiny is written in the stars. Based on this myth, our destinies depend on the position of the constellations at the time we were born. For thousands of years, people have believed in this myth. Another interesting myth says that your destiny is written on your palm. It is also a well-developed subject that tries to read your destiny according to the lines on your hand.

If we accept the premise that destiny is predetermined, simple logic says that you don't have to do anything in life. You would simply become who you are destined to be. This would also indicate that we as humans don't have choices in our lives, which is not the case. If we didn't have choices, we wouldn't be human. The rest of the living organisms are unable to make a choice. Therefore, destiny is simply a product of your choices and actions.

A Mathematical Equation

 To control your destiny, you need to understand the factors that affect it and manage those factors.

All of us know about mathematical equations. They have two components: factors and an end result. The end result is a product of different factors. Depending on which factors are in the equation, the end result can differ.

Destiny is the same concept. It is a product of various factors in our lives. Most of the time, we associate the outcome with only one or two factors. We rarely think that there might be several factors influencing the outcome. It is your understanding of the different factors that enables you to control your destiny. In life, when we have a problem, we usually try to take the first solution. However, as humans, we are born with the ability to be creative, the greatest tool we have to control our destinies. How does creativity help? Every problem has a solution. When one factor of the equation cannot be altered, another factor can help us arrive at the desired outcome.

 Use your creativity to control your destiny.

Creativity helps us identify the other factors and determine different solutions to the problem. Before you solve a problem, you need to gather as many ideas as possible. It is a numbers game. No matter how ridiculous or great the ideas are, you need as many ideas as possible for different factors of the equation. Once you have different ideas, then you can decide on one or two ideas to solve the problem. To generate as many ideas as possible, you need to turn on your creativity. Sounds too technical? Let's bring it to real life.

Controlling Your Destiny

How do you apply this thinking to real life? It is very easy. The following process gives you an outline:

1. **Define your destiny.** Know where you want to be in life. Do you want to be a CEO? Or do you just want to be happy with what you have? Think about what result will satisfy you. However, try not to think about achieving this end result in this step. For example, if you are working in lower ranks and getting by day to day, making a million dollars might seem like a ridiculous idea in the current state. However, if you want to make a million dollars, you first need to strategize and take action. So before you strategize, define what you want to achieve.

2. **Strategize.** Strategize how you want to achieve it. Strategy is how you go about achieving anything in life. Life is all about strategy. Strategizing is a process where you find all the factors that influence your destiny and arrive at a plan to control them.

3. **Commit.** Once you strategize, make a commitment every day to achieve your strategy and your goals. Spend a few minutes out of your busy life achieving your dreams. The time you spend on that will be much more fulfilling than the adrenaline rush of doing urgent things.

4. **Start.** Once you strategize, just start working on it. Journeying to the moon begins with the first step toward the rocket.

5. **Persistence, persistence, persistence.** Once you start, you have to keep at it. You will always face obstacles. Plans never go as planned. However, you should never lose sight of your goal. If you have the persistence, you will alter the plan or keep at the plan to achieve your goal. In a practical sense, once you start applying your strategy in the first couple of weeks, you will be excited. After about three weeks, it will become a routine. Also, you might go through a difficult patch in your life and not get a chance to look at your goals. Just keep a reminder in your calendar or on the fridge to revisit and revive your goals. Get back into your plan and keep at it. Getting back to a strategy is better than abandoning a strategy. Finish what you started, as long as the end goal still makes sense to you.

Conclusion

Destiny is something that is within your control. Controlling destiny is about identifying the factors that influence our final destinies and changing them to get the outcomes we want. Strategy is the key to that control. It allows us to get at our dreams through little steps every day. There is never a dream that you cannot achieve.

CHAPTER 5

STRATEGIZING YOUR
CAREER AND LIFE

L ife is all about strategy. How we strategize our lives determines how successful we become. Strategy is a subject generally taught in business schools and associated with managing corporations. Yet our everyday lives are filled with opportunities when applying strategy becomes a crucial requirement. The distinction between success and failure boils down to the strategy that we use in these situations. Strategy can be defined as follows:

> **Strategy:**
> The approach you take to close the gap between where you are and where you want to be.

 We need to consciously strategize our success.

Though this is a broad definition, it essentially means that we need to consciously plan the approach we take to achieve our goals. As simple as it sounds, very few people actually take this approach. It is a skill that has to be developed. The world around us has been built because people strategized and executed on their strategies. How much we consciously strategize defines our successes and failures. There are many business books written about the subject of strategy. To put it simply, strategy is your "approach" to your goal.

 Strategy brings choices into action.

Strategy is the primary tool for success. It is with strategy that you can get hold of destiny and make it happen. In your arsenal of tools for success, strategy should be the one that will help you most. It is what brings choices into action. The reasons for strategizing are numerous, but here are a few of the top reasons why you need to master it.

- Achieving big dreams is difficult and complex. Having a strategy in place helps turn each of your dreams into reality. Dreams always are high-level ideas. For most, dreams remain dreams because it is very difficult to bring them down to a day-to-day level. Instead, we would rather be doing urgent and unimportant tasks, such as vacuuming the floor or changing tires on the car rather than working on dreams. Strategy enables us to bring our dreams to the level of other day-to-day realities.

- One of the main challenges we have with goals and aspirations is knowing the next logical steps needed to achieve them. When goals become complex, knowing the next logical step becomes very difficult. As a result, we put off most of our goals. To make anything happen, you need to know the next logical step. Strategy helps us determine the next logical step.

- Strategy becomes an action plan to achieve your goals. Once you have a breakdown of the next things to do, you can then add details around each action step. You even can further strategize each step in your overall strategy. Once you are finished, you will have an action plan to execute.

- Most important, once you have each of the subsequent tasks broken down and planned out, you will have the confidence that your dreams are in fact achievable. This is something that differentiates most high performers from the rest because high performers believe that anything is achievable. They have the confidence to work on goals and dreams. You will have the same confidence because you will have a plan in place to make your dreams come true.

 You can break down your dreams into more manageable parts by strategizing.

Most of us put off our dreams. The sheer size of our dreams and their complexity are often what deter us from acting on them. Subconsciously, we fear complex projects and actions, though we justify our procrastination with other reasons at a conscious level. As a result, most of our dreams go unaccomplished in our lifetimes. We start believing dreams are just dreams. Contrarily, I believe that dreams can be reality. You need only to give good thought to making them reality. Strategy enables us to do this. Strategy breaks down our dreams into manageable chunks that we can visualize, feel, and execute on a day-to-day basis, just as we would do laundry or go to the grocery store.

Everyday tasks are easy to do because we can see them, feel them, and we know what their outcome will be. Strategy brings your dreams to this level, which is extremely powerful.

Right now, the dream of owning a dream house, becoming a millionaire, or becoming a CEO might seem like something out of this world. You might be even embarrassed to talk about it fearing that your friends and family will write you off as a dreamer. But, if you have the right strategy in place and keep working on it, I am telling you that your dreams are achievable. They are as real as the shirt on your back.

Stop for a second and think about how you would approach a journey to a friend's place that you don't know the way to.

1. First and foremost, you know that you have to go to your friend's place—you have a goal!

2. You need to figure out how to get there. Are you going to ask another friend, or are you going to look at a map? This is your strategy.

3. You decide the route (select your strategy).

4. Finally, you take the road, follow the turns, and complete the trip (strategy implementation/execution).

I know this sound like common sense. This is the natural thinking process that would take place in approaching any task. Our limitation is that we rarely apply this process to complex tasks and the goals we want to achieve. It is easy to have goals; it is equally important to have a strategy to achieve these goals.

Everything that we do in life requires an approach, from brushing your teeth in the morning to building a skyscraper. The difference between a normal person and a high performer is that a high performer knows how to approach complex goals, i.e., strategize. High performers consciously strategize their goals.

Learning how to strategize is crucial for the success of your career.

Strategy is a very simple skill. The higher you go up the corporate ladder, the less technical you get. One of the few skills that remain with you is your ability to strategize. Leaders at the top of any corporation know the principles of strategy and know how to apply them, while employees at lower levels know the principles but don't know how to apply them. When it comes to life, you need to start thinking like a CEO.

You would not be able to get up in the morning and come to work if you didn't know how to strategize. As humans, strategy is how we think. It is a natural process for us. However, CEOs know how to consciously apply this ordinary skill to very complex problems and attain large goals. This is what we are going to learn in this chapter.

To succeed, you need to spend enough time strategizing and fine-tuning the strategy.

One of the prime reasons that our plans fail is we don't spend enough time strategizing and fine-tuning our strategy. A goal is not the same as a strategy. Just because you have a goal does not mean you have a plan. You need to have a strategy for each goal. When you do, then you can break down the strategy into individual tasks and execution plans. This is part of strategy formulation.

When you don't have a strategy, you are more reluctant to approach complex problems.

Have you ever wanted to lose, say, 50 pounds? Each year, you make a New Year's resolution to lose the excess weight. And at the end of each year, you have little or no success. One of the reasons you are in the same place is you haven't strategized your weight-loss goal. When you don't have a strategy, you are more reluctant to approach any complex problem, primarily because you don't know how to approach the goal; so you put it off.

For a long time I was seeking the answer on how to achieve great goals. I was very ambitious. I wanted to achieve great things. I read a lot of books on time management, organizing, and how to get things done. I didn't find the answer that I was looking for. I found everything *around* what I was looking for, but I didn't find the core answer I wanted.

To be great, you have to get things done. To do great things, you have to set goals and organize your time. But what was missing in all those books was *how* to strategize on achieving these goals. Strategizing on achieving great things is something that each of us needs to do. We can set goals and learn a spectrum of techniques, but if we don't know how to apply the techniques to achieve goals, we don't get anywhere.

Sometimes strategy comes to us by sheer chance.

Sometimes, strategy comes to us by sheer chance. One thing might lead to another, and you have a strategy in place. Whether in the business world or the personal, strategy happens a lot by chance. We find out that something is working out for us and we start going down a certain path. A lot of us take this route. But, of course, you're leaving your destiny to chance.

There is actually no formula for strategy. Each goal is unique. With strategy, there is almost no formula or procedure to apply. We need to figure out how to get from point A to point B. The strategic framework certainly helps to formulate the strategy.

Each of our dreams and goals is different. They are as personal to you as your personality. Each of your goals will differ from the next in terms of its complexity, time required to achieve, difficulty, and circumstances. Each goal and dream should be governed by its own set of criteria. Because of this complexity, it is impossible to have one formula to strategize your goals. If you encounter a prescription for achieving your goals, be skeptical because no two goals are the same, whether they are yours or those of two different people. You can never prescribe a formula to achieve your goals.

However, when working on your goals and dreams, you will notice that the approach has similar components, no matter how big or small your goal is. These components are common to your approach whether you are trying to go from your house to dinner or you are trying to grow a multinational bank from $60 billion profitability to $100 billion profitability. Based on these components, we can build a framework for you to strategize your goals and, ultimately, your dreams.

These components in the framework are the primary components of any plan. Yes, strategy is a plan. They form logical steps to breaking down any problem and executing a plan to solve it. In fact, these components form the logical thinking process in the human brain. Skipping any one of the steps would make it difficult for you to achieve your goals. We use this approach on a daily basis. The only difference is that we are going to use these steps consciously rather than subconsciously.

The steps in the framework are interrelated. They are in logical order, and each is dependent on the previous. Most of the time, this planning process becomes recursive as well, which means that steps within the strategy might become strategies themselves. You need to strategize complex goals at different levels. Each level is a strategy on its own.

In the example below, as a VP, you will need to strategize how to get a promotion at each level. These ideas, these subcomponents, will combine to become a collection of strategies.

In the world of software design, this is the same approach used to build complex software programs such as operating systems and transaction-processing systems. Before a single line of code is written, the very first step is to break down the design objectives into the different major components. These major components are then given to different teams that go and break down the major components into even smaller components. They are planned to the most minute detail. Only in the final step does the code get written.

Your dreams are similarly complex. This is why it is important to break down the actions into smaller steps to ensure the execution of your plans. The strategic framework will help you to do this with your goals and dreams.

Strategy in Detail

There are many definitions of strategy. In the world of business, strategy is a concept that many management gurus have written about. Some definitions claim that strategy is an art for devising plans, while others refer to strategy as a more structured approach. Whichever definition you prefer, strategy is about achieving goals and planning.

A Strategic Planning Framework is about taking common concepts in strategy and applying them to your personal life.

When we think about doing something, we essentially need to answer five questions: what, why, when, where, and how. "What" is the actual goal itself. It is the target. For example, you might want to obtain your MBA. "What" refers to earning an MBA as your goal. Once you've answered the "What" question, you need to answer the "Why." For you to have a goal, you obviously must know why you want something. The questions "when" and "where" are your tactics for achieving your goal. "How" is your strategy.

Having read many definitions of strategy, I like to think of strategy simply as the approach to achieving goals. It answers the question "How do I achieve a goal?" How to achieve a goal is the next question to ask after you know what you want to achieve and why you want to achieve it. It follows the same natural thinking pattern in our brain, and it is a very important component.

Similar to the different definitions of strategy, there are different versions of defining a plan. However, most of these versions have five primary components (which I will cover later on in the chapter).

These components answer the what, why, when, where, and how questions. This framework is what I call a Strategic Planning Framework, something that can be applied to any problem, goal, or dream that you have.

It is sometimes easy to confuse strategy and tactics. Sometimes, tactics in a large plan might turn out to be smaller strategies themselves. Yet it is important to keep strategy and tactics separate. In order to solve complex problems, you need to know the difference between strategy and tactics. When devising a plan, think first about strategy and then about tactics. In each plan, the level of planning is different. Thus, your definition of strategy and tactics will be different for each plan. When planning, you need to know at what level your strategy starts to become tactical. In order to solve complex problems, you need to know the difference between the two.

The action items for your strategy are the lowest level of your plan. They are not necessarily your tactics. Once you start breaking down the work required to achieve your goals; you will come to a point where you cannot divide them further. In your dream of becoming a CEO, your tactic might be to get a job at the next level. Completing your resume for that next-level job is an action that you cannot break down further. It is steps as small as these that constitute your action plan. Typically, individual actions take less than one hour to complete. Thus, your tactics might not be your action items. You might need to further strategize and break down each tactic until you know the individual action items.

 When devising strategy, you might not be able to see every activity at the onset. This is normal.

When devising your strategy, it is likely that you won't be able to foresee most of your tactics at their individual task level. Do not worry too much about it because it is typical in devising strategy. As long as you have the approach and the next immediate steps required to strategize your dream, you have a good strategy. What is important is the next step that is required. Always having a firm idea of the next few steps that will keep you moving. Not knowing the next step and not giving adequate thought to it is what keeps people away from their dreams. You can elaborate as you move through your strategy.

Once you have a strategy in place, it becomes a project. Projects typically get elaborated on as you move through the project. This means that the details for the strategy become clearer as you move closer to those steps and tactics. Life is full of uncertainty, and plans have to be changed. This is why it is important to elaborate on your strategy as you move on, when the circumstances for each step become clear. As you go on, what you planned just a few weeks ago might change. You need to account for this uncertainty. You achieve this through continuous elaboration.

As should be clear now, strategy is the process of taking what you want to achieve and breaking it down to a level that becomes actionable. The hierarchy of a strategy can be illustrated as follows:

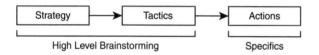

As we go down the hierarchy, we add the details. Only once we determine the actions can we start adding the specifics such as when and how to do these actions.

Even if you look at your strategy over time, the window in which you will have the specifics is quite narrow.

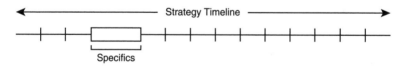

Though you might know the specifics only for your current window of work that you are doing, you will have an idea of what high-level activities need to take place.

Goals are often problems that need solutions. Strategy is your solution to the problem and tactics are how you go about implementing the solution to the problem.

Application of strategy can be best illustrated by example. Let's make a plan.

Situation

I'm currently a junior financial analyst. I want to be successful in my career and make a difference in my day-to-day work. Therefore, I want to become a vice president (VP) of finance for my company. A financial analyst is a level 6 in the corporation, and a VP is a level 11. A move from one level to another represents a promotion.

Goal/Problem

I want to become a vice president (VP).

Data

There are several promotions required to become a VP.

I am currently a level 6, and a VP is a level 11.

I want to become a VP by the time I am 42 years old.

I am 29 right now.

Requirements for promotions at each level are different.

Strategy

Get promoted from level to level.

Set target timeframes and work toward initiating each promotion.

Be proactive in working toward each promotion.

At each level, strategize the next promotion.

Have contingency plans, as the right opportunities might not come.

At each level, develop the requirements for the next level.

Tactics

Focus on promotion to a senior financial analyst (level 7) by the time I am 30 years old.

To achieve a level 7, I have to be technically very competent.

Develop the technical competency.

Focus on getting promoted.

Talk to my manager about what I need to develop to achieve this promotion.

After achieving level 7, restrategize for level 8.

As you can see, strategy is your approach to attaining your goals. As a junior financial analyst, you might have felt it was impossible to become a VP. However, by having an approach, I managed to break the problem down into smaller problems. After I achieved the first sub-goal, the ultimate goal of becoming a VP seemed more and more plausible. Tactics such as developing individual skills and competencies now fit into the total picture.

Another way to look at strategy is to think of it as the framework. Think of the human body. The spine or backbone holds everything upright. Everything else connects to the backbone. Your strategy is like the backbone of your plan. Everything else connects to this strategy. Once you know your strategy, you know what areas you need to focus on and what areas not to focus on. It is easier to solve any problem if you first think of the strategy.

Importance of Strategy and Strategic Planning

Strategy is the difference between success and failure. Without a good approach to a problem and a firm action plan, there would not be a solution. Your approach is your solution to the problem. This is why strategy is very important in our lives.

 Strategy is the 80/20 principle in practice.

Thus, it is important to get your strategy correct before you proceed with your most important goals. If the strategy is not correct, attaining the goal is going to be a very difficult task. Compared to the time you spend working at your goals, the time taken to strategize is minimal, yet it is the step that has the greatest effect. Once you strategize, you will head in the correct direction toward the goal. Strategizing is the 80/20 principle in practice—you spend 20 percent of your time strategizing and planning, but it represents 80 percent of the work toward your goal. Strategy is the backbone of any goal. Once the strategy is correct, handling the tactics and the details will be an easy task.

To gain momentum on your strategy, you need to overcome the emotional resistance.

Most of the effort involved in attaining your goal is overcoming the emotional resistance. Once you start and engage in making your dreams a reality, you go with the flow. Overcoming this emotional resistance is what we achieve by strategizing. Though it does not require an ounce of physical effort, our emotional selves keep us away from our dreams. We like our dreams, but the sheer detail of them keeps us away.

By front loading the thinking and strategizing, we overcome this emotional barrier. Though thinking is less than 20 percent of the effort involved, it is the most difficult part. The more time spent thinking about how you are going to execute this strategy and the more detail and specifics that you can outline, the easier it makes the execution. The 20 percent effort might actually feel like 80 percent of the effort because this is actually the part that we resist most when trying to achieve something.

By thinking through the details, we know what to expect with the realities of the strategy. For example, you might think you can do a certain job, such as senior financial analyst, but once you think through the specifics, you realize that before you get to senior financial analyst, you need to gain more confidence. This might require you to become a financial analyst for two years before you even attempt to become a senior financial analyst. It is very important to be realistic about the details. While dreams might not be realistic, we have to be realistic with the details of achieving them.

Successful people don't call their dreams unrealistic. For them, dreams are realistic. But when it comes to actions, they know what is unrealistic and what is not. This is why strategy is so important. Strategy will give you the realism required to achieve your vision. It brings your vision to reality.

Every one of us has challenges that need solutions. For you it could be marriage, a financial situation, a time-management problem, or simply your physical shape. All our lives have challenges. In order to solve these problems and challenges, we need strategies. With a Strategic Planning Framework, we can start to break down these problems into solutions. This is why strategic planning is crucial in our lives.

We need to think within the Strategic Planning Framework, especially when our challenges are complex. Our human brains sometimes have difficulty breaking down complex problems. A framework helps us break down a problem into manageable parts. The Strategic Planning Framework works the same way.

The Strategic Planning Framework is like a lever or a set of pulleys. We apply the same level of thinking to complex problems that we apply to simple problems. It helps us isolate the approach.

How Do You Strategize?

Strategizing is not a new skill. We all know how to strategize. What we need to learn is how to apply the same framework that we are familiar with to more complex problems. When there is a complex problem, strategizing skills do not come as naturally to us. We need a framework that will take us along the correct path.

A Strategic Planning Framework is a framework to plan your goals. The framework will guide your thinking toward a strategy rather than a list of action items. It will help you think about complex problems and attain complex goals in your life.

You might be able to follow this thought process without any writing. However, for more complex goals, it is best to write down your thoughts in each section to create a record of your strategy. This way, you can always refer to it at a future date. Sometimes goals take awhile to achieve.

Strategic Planning Framework

The framework consists of five thought components, or processes.

Definition: Defines and visualizes what you want to achieve.

Data/Analysis: What you know about the situation.

Strategy: How you want to achieve your goal.

Tactics/Resources: What has to be done to execute the strategy.

Monitoring: How to ensure you're successful.

Definition: Write down the problem that you are trying to solve and the goal. This will act as a reference point for your planning. For example, your problem could be your current level of debt and the goal would be to get out of debt completely. Or it could be that you are not satisfied with your current salary and want to get to a higher position.

Writing down the problem will remind you why you are trying to attain the goal. It will provide a purpose for the effort. Sometimes we forget our purpose for doing something. Often we lose the motivation to go toward a goal when we lose sight of the purpose. Writing down the problem helps prevent this.

There are also times when we want to attain a goal but have not really thought about why. For the longest time, I've wanted to become a CEO and never gave a thought to why. Using the framework, I now understand why.

Knowing what motivates you and understanding the reason behind your goals will give you a lot of clarity. For example, I might want to become a CEO. What motivated me to become a CEO is to make a difference. By articulating the reason for my goal, I realized that there are other ways, not just through becoming a CEO. As you can see, by defining your goal, you will really be able to understand what you are trying to achieve. It also will assist you in selecting the most appropriate path to achieve your goal.

Defining and visualizing the end state of your dream has a profound impact on its success.

Defining your goal is about knowing your end state. Even if your goal is complex, it is imperative that you know what your end state looks like. Many authors have written about visualizing your end state. When you can visualize and feel your end state as if it is here today with you, it becomes a powerful motivation to achieve your goal.

I have a wonderful story that illustrates the principles of visualizing and strategizing. In 2008, in the middle of the financial crisis, a good friend of mine was on the brink of going bankrupt. As he was a good friend of mine, I had told him awhile ago about the technique of visualization. He was actually contemplating whether to declare bankruptcy. Everything was going wrong. He was told that his job might be eliminated, probably in the coming four months. He was working for a large North American bank, the worst type of place to be employed at that time. He was heavily in debt but had savings to offset that debt invested in the stock market. Then the stock market took a huge nosedive. Within a week, most of his money was wiped out. His efforts to get financing failed because the banks weren't lending. He had only enough money to feed his family for a week, but not enough to pay the mortgage and bills. He was living a lavish life, and it was a massive blow to his ego and self-worth. Many people went through that during that year. He admitted that his own bad financial management, lavish spending, and unfortunate circumstances all caved in on his family at the same time.

Yet he used the visualizing technique to visualize his end state. He visualized a state of being financially healthy and stable every morning. He defined exactly what he wants to be. It meant having a stable job and at least one year worth of savings so that he could weather any future financial emergency. Most would have laughed at him if they heard his definition statement given where he was in reality. He would have been called a dreamer. Because he was able to define his end state, however, he was able to work every day on something to improve his financial situation. He turned around his situation in an amazing way. He knew he couldn't solve this problem with the same mindset that created it. He turned around his spending and his savings outlook. He worked hard in his job and proved to his management that he could do more than he was hired to do. It was hard at first. It was very difficult at first. Within a year, together with his wife, they had six months' worth of savings (which is a lot better than none); he was one of the few to be retained and had no credit card debt. He spent a lot less, and his life is lot more frugal now. His family doesn't love the way they spend money now compared with one year ago, but they are in far better shape than they were a year ago. Even with the spending that he did over the year, he has achieved a lot and has things to show for it. His example was a textbook turnaround case. To turn around his financial state that way required amazing discipline, which I admire. When he told his story to me, I was amazed.

 Every day, make it a habit to write down what your end states look like for your dreams. It works!

Many would call his turnaround a miracle. I attribute it to clearly defining his goal and working every day to achieve it. You need to do something to achieve your goal every day. You can do it once you clearly define it. Every morning, the first thing I do when I get up is write down my goal and plan on what I can do to move one step closer to it, however small the step. I write down my end state as if I have it today. I don't tell anyone what I write because it would sound ridiculous to an outsider. No doubt I would be called a dreamer. But the amazing thing is that it works! My biggest problem is keeping my list current because everything seems to come true. I have to keep revising this list because I keep on achieving my goals. Knowing the end state and constantly reminding yourself where you want to be is the very first step to attaining it.

Data/Analysis: Write down what you already know about the problem or the goal, any analysis you've done to determine the problem, and any assumptions. This will help you strategize better as you will decide which data to consider. Furthermore, this will help remind you later on what assumptions you have made when strategizing.

Another piece of information that needs to be recorded here is your Critical Success Factors. Critical Success Factors are what need to be done to ensure the success of the goal. For example, if you want to become a VP, it is critical for you to maintain an excellent track record of credibility.

Critical Success Factors determine the outcome of your strategy.

Knowing your Critical Success Factors is important. There will be a lot of things in your plan of attack that might or might not be critical. But you need to understand what is critical and focus your energy on those activities. Critical activities are activities that make or break your strategy. These activities have to be done well in order for your strategy to be successful. You need to work very hard to address the factors that will be critical for your strategy. Working on critical factors can be difficult. It requires you to push yourself beyond your comfort zone. But if you don't get the critical aspects of your strategy worked out, your strategy will sit in limbo for a long time.

In my friend's financial situation, his first critical factor was to pull together some money until he could sort out the situation. He had to go to his family for a loan. The next critical factor was for him to rethink his entire spending habits and bring discipline to his spending. Though he had a budget previously, he had never followed this budget. It meant brown bagging his lunch, going to the discount stores rather than the flashy grocery stores, and really thinking through the purpose of each dollar that he spent. The next critical factor was building up his savings. For that, he started contributing 10 percent of his gross income to a savings plan that he could not touch. Fortunately for him, his company had the ability to do that. The final critical factor was to follow frugal spending patterns on a continuous basis and make them a habit. Every time he got paid, he made it a point to sit down first thing in the morning to pay off all his bills, bucket his financials, and reconcile everything. By identifying your critical factors, you will be able to focus on what is most important in your strategy.

Strategy: This is the important section that requires a lot of thinking. After knowing the problem and goal, you need to think of an approach to attaining the goal. This is the solution to the problem. However, you don't have to worry about the details of the solution at this point. Just think about the high-level solution. How would you approach the goal? That is the question that you have to answer.

To strategize, you need to harness the creative self within you.

Sometimes you might arrive at several different solutions or approaches to attaining the goal. Don't be judgmental; just write them down. The moment you become judgmental, you lose the creativity required in the process. Strategy creation is a very creative exercise. Don't worry if you think you are not creative. Creativity for strategic thinking is in all of us. The only thing we have to do is harness it. Learning to harness the creativity is a skill that can be learned very easily.

Society tells us to subdue our creativity in different ways. Becoming risk averse is one way of subduing creativity. At the same time, we sometimes fear the acceptance of one of our ideas. Because of this fear, we become very judgmental about our ideas. When we are strategizing, we need to turn this self-editor off for a moment.

Be creative and generate as many ideas as possible. Once you have exhausted all the possible approaches, you can decide on the best solution later on. The idea is to brainstorm as many solutions as possible.

Strategizing is all about creating. All of us have the ability to create, but very few of us let our imaginative mind create things. Generating ideas for your strategy requires you to let your mind run free. We teach our children how to do this, but as adults we hardly do it ourselves. I was amazed to see that these very concepts that I am writing about were in a children's show my four-year-old daughter was watching, yet when we really need them, we rarely use these basic skills that we have. When we were children, we all learned these things, but life got to us and overshadowed them. We need to go back to them, because that is what we need to be successful.

You need to be creative and generate ideas. We need to think as much as possible. Let your mind run free and generate as many ideas as possible. You have to stop evaluating them. It is then that your mind starts running free. The process of evaluating and judging your ideas when you get them actually hinders this process. I know it will take training when you are not used to doing it. Once you are used to generating ideas, keep going. Your mind will give you lots of ideas. Don't stop, write them down, and go on till you have exhausted all your thinking. Let your creative self come to life.

To be a good strategist, you need to make yourself an artist. Artists let their minds run free. They don't judge the ideas they get, and they don't evaluate what comes to their mind. They express these ideas on whatever work they are doing. There is no dampening effect between their idea creation and action. This is what you need when you are generating your ideas. There should not be any dampening. You would be amazed by the fabulous ideas that you can generate, no matter what you think of yourself. When you let your mind run free, it takes on a life of its own, and it will give you fabulous material to work with.

Once we have a list of ideas and options, we need to start evaluating each of our ideas in a very objective manner for the best solution. We need to select one idea out of the list. The criteria for selecting the best course of action could be anything.

When your list of ideas is in front of you, you can then start evaluating them. This is the time when you start judging your ideas by weighing the pros and the cons of each.

The criterion for selecting could be what appeals to you most. It could be the most financially viable solution or the fastest solution. It also could be a combination of criteria with different priorities. Whatever the criterion is, you need to pick the one that feels most right for you. There are many problems and solutions in life that you can never measure quantitatively. People who hide behind reams of analysis will never make decisions. They just fear taking responsibility by making a decision. Selecting the solution and moving forward is the most important thing they will do.

 It is very important that you make a choice rather than hiding behind analysis.

This is the time when you need to make a decision. The choice that you make will define you. You cannot hide behind reams of quantitative analysis. You need to take a risk and move forward. I have had conversations with people who buy houses who come to me for advice. It amazes me how much analysis they do before they buy.

Some measure the distance from the public transit in minutes and seconds and even calculate the heating bill. While I agree that you need analysis to make an informed decision, I also have the feeling that they are just frightened to make a decision, take the risk, and be responsible for their decision.

You need to make a choice that will make you happy. These are your dreams. I'm not against quantitative analysis, and it *is* required before taking a giant leap. But you need to trust your gut and select the idea that will make you happy. It all boils down to your purpose. It is very important that you make this connection.

When I was considering whether to buy my current house, I decided that as long as I could afford it and my gut agreed with the decision, I should go for it. I needed to be happy in that house. As a result, I always got the house I wanted and never regretted a single decision.

You can sense when you are about to make the correct choice. You just need to trust that feeling and make that choice. The choice that you make is usually the correct choice. I know you would have that edgy feeling that this could be the wrong choice. But contrary to that feeling at the time of making it, I have always experienced that the choice I made is the best possible choice I could have made. I have a wonderful life today because I do that and I trust myself.

Tactics/Resources: Once you select the best solution to your problem or the best approach, you can add the beef to it. You can start answering the questions such as when, where, and how. Tactics are the smaller details of your plan.

 Once you have your approach identified, you can then add the details.

It is great to think about the approach. However, you also need to think about the smaller details of the plan in order to implement it. Most of the time, when we get great ideas, we fail to implement them.

In most strategies, the difference between strategy and tactics is a very fine line. It is often a gray area. Don't worry if you have difficulty differentiating strategy and tactics. In such situations, think of both the strategy and tactics as one unit.

Most of the time, we fail to think through the details of the idea. Thinking through the details requires us to do two things:

1. Evaluate the feasibility of the idea.
2. Think through the implementation tasks.

Because we fail to think through these two aspects, one of two things happens that makes us procrastinate. We either feel reluctant to start working on it because we don't know how to go about the task, making us anxious about the goal, or we underestimate how much work the task is going to be. As a result, the task ends up being a failure as we put too little time and energy into it.

While strategy is important for us, it is also important to think through the details behind the strategy and the idea.

Let us take an example of thinking through the details. You want to renovate your kitchen. Strategy would be to first work on the floor and then the cabinets. You have decided on the design of the cupboards. You are going to do it in three months' time, and you have decided to limit the spending to $5,000.

Now let us think through a few of the details. Since this is a large project, let's take just a component—the floor. First you need to know what tools you would need, and then you need to figure out how to obtain the tools. If they are going to cost you something, they must be part of the budget. Then think about where you are going to purchase the tiles and how you are going to bring them home. Do you rent a truck, or can you manage with your car? Similarly, think through the details.

The best way to think about the tactics is to visualize what you are doing before you actually do it. This not only helps you to find answers to the two things but it also helps you to prepare mentally for the things that you are going to do. This is going to save a lot of time when you are doing it, as you will know what you are going to do.

In the same process, you also need to think through the resources you will need: things such as money, nails, and people.

Don't worry if you don't have all the details correctly nailed down. There will be things that you will not know. Also don't delay starting because you don't know all the details. There will be things that you'll have to think about once you start. The idea is to start and not to hide behind the details. You need to use the details to help you get started, not as a hiding place from starting. Even if we do manage to get all these details correct, most of us still hide behind the details to avoid starting. We are scared to start a new venture.

Once you get most of your details, you can start executing the plan.

Monitoring: While having plans and tactics is good, we also need to monitor how we progress in these plans. You need to step back and see how things are going. There would be no way for us to know whether we are progressing well if we don't compare against our original goal. Most of the time, we get so caught up in the day-to-day urgent tasks and put off the important strategies and plans. When this happens, we delay achieving our goals. So it is important to sit down and consciously monitor how we are doing against the plan.

It could be that you have to make changes to the time line. For example, say you had a goal of losing 20 pounds this year; it is already September, and you have lost only 5 pounds. You need to accelerate your weight loss or else rethink your goal. You might need to look again at the tactics and adopt a more aggressive set of tactics to increase your weight loss.

Maybe you require a complete change in direction. You might discover that going down this path is simply not feasible, even though you thought initially that it was going to work out. So now you have to think about the overall strategy and restrategize.

 Plans and strategy will change. Again, this is normal.

Don't be afraid to make changes to your plans. The idea is to move forward in the things that you do. If the plan and strategy that you made is taking you backward, then you have to restrategize. As normal as it is to have plans, it is also normal to change plans. When you are making plans, you rarely know all the details. This is why changing plans is important. The fact that what you are doing is taking you to a better place and is making you happier is the most important thing. Strategies and plans are ways of fulfilling your dreams and aspirations. It helps to think of achieving these dreams in a structured way. However, just because you made a plan does not mean that you have to stick with that dream if the dream does not work out.

There are times when changing plans also does not work. Sometimes keeping at the plan is what you need. This is not a formula-based determination. It should be based on individual circumstances. If you know that the goal you are trying to achieve is the right thing to do, and you are convinced the strategy is the correct approach, then keep at the same strategy. Persistence is very important when you are convinced that you are doing the right thing. The whole world might disagree with you, but if you are convinced that you are doing the right thing, then you have to keep at it.

Conclusion

Though this whole process seems complicated, everything in life is strategized using the same natural process. Strategy is our natural way of thinking. When our brain cannot apply the same thinking pattern to more complex problems, we need to help the brain to apply the thinking process to more complex problems. We need to help the brain do what it does well—think. The framework helps you do that. It puts more complex problems in reach of the brain. Think of it as a lever. You can use bare hands to lift light weights. Our brains are built in the same way—to do light thinking. Similarly, when lifting heavy weights, we don't lift with our bare hands, we use pulleys, chains, and levers. However, we still apply the same pressure and principles, but we are lifting a much heavier object using the tools. This framework is a similar tool. It is not new. We are just taking it to the next level. By using the framework, we are assisting the brain in applying the same level of thinking to more complex tasks.

I have read a lot of books on time management. They talk about a lot of goal setting, tactics, and techniques to manage your time. However, I have yet to come across a time-management book that talks about strategizing the things that you have to do. The essence of time management is to make the most of our lives. In order to do this, you need to have a strategy for each goal. Most time-management gurus in fact miss the core essence of time management by failing to talk about strategy. Without an approach, you would not know how to go about a goal.

Strategy is the core of getting things done. Everything in life can be strategized. You don't have to own a business or be a CEO to know about strategy.

Using the framework above is like breaking a stack of sticks. If you try to break the whole stack at once, you will never achieve it. However, you break one stick at a time; you will then be able to break the whole stack. The Strategic Planning Framework helps you do exactly that.

CHAPTER 6

BEING PROACTIVE

Proactive people become successful. On your road to success, one of the key skills you need to learn is to be proactive. The proactive person is ahead in almost every aspect of life. It is one of the essential skills that differentiate the high performers from the rest. It enables you to anticipate the things that will happen and be prepared.

Being proactive means to actively participate, anticipate various permutations in our plans, and influence the change toward our goals. This is an important trait that is found in most high performers. High performers are people who are very good at reading the future and influencing it. They are prepared to act on opportunities before others. If you are the first to capitalize on an opportunity, you will get the most out of that opportunity.

Being proactive gives you the chance to get ahead. Though you might not know what the future holds for you, being proactive helps you to prepare for the events and the opportunities that come your way.

Another argument for being proactive is to influence the change you need. You won't have control of all the factors that drive your success, but you can certainly influence them. You need to be able to take control of your future by doing what you can to influence it.

What Does It Mean to Be Proactive?

Learn to read the future and be prepared for it.

Quite simply, being proactive means to actively participate and anticipate opportunities: being prepared for all the opportunities that come your way and staying focused on your goal regardless of the obstacles and the unplanned events.

Being proactive is being prepared for known as well as unknown events so that you can capitalize on and handle every situation efficiently and effectively. It is about anticipating every permutation on the road toward your goal and making sure that nothing keeps you from achieving your goal.

It is about planning for contingencies. Contingencies are possible deviations from the goal. If you are a project manager, you know about this very well. Projects are all about achieving a specific objective, just like life goals. To achieve a project's objective, a project manager will plan for all the contingencies that he or she can think of.

In the world of business, if you are not proactive, your competition will eat you alive. Companies such as IBM (not anticipating the rise of the personal computer) and Kodak (not anticipating the digital camera) are case studies in how not being proactive can kill a profitable business. These principles can be applied to real life. Sometimes, life should be run like a business.

Why Should You Be Proactive?

The first benefit of being prepared is better quality of results and better quality of life. When we set goals, we all want to achieve a quality result. What is quality? Quality is essentially achieving what we expected from doing the project or the task. We all know that what we expect does not always happen. In order to achieve what we expect, we need to anticipate things that could go wrong and be prepared for them. By doing this preparation, we can achieve our goals according to our expectations. Being proactive thus leads to a quality life.

You need to anticipate competitive forces and be prepared to tackle these forces.

In your journey toward success, you will always face competition from other people. By preparing yourself in competitive situations, you will always have an edge. People who are better prepared always make it first. Most others are usually not prepared. It is in our nature to push things until the last moment. It is rare that people consciously plan for and anticipate problems. At the same time, by being prepared for different opportunities, you can capture those opportunities before others even know that there are opportunities. Luck is when opportunity meets preparation. You will always be ahead of the curve by being prepared.

By being prepared, you eliminate stress. Stress is a fact of life. We always get stressed, no matter how competent we are. It is how we manage it that differentiates the high performers from the rest. Stress is primarily a physical reaction to situations that we are unable to control. Some work well under stress, but most of us don't. It has very harmful effects on our health. So we need to manage it as much as possible. One of the key ways to control your level of stress is to be prepared. When you set a goal, you know things are going to go wrong. There will hardly be a plan in this world that will not have any obstacles. Think through these obstacles, from the most remote to the most likely deviations. Then plan for them so that when these events happen, it will be very easy to correct the situation.

Being proactive builds your confidence.

On the same note, being proactive gives you confidence. Your confidence has a tremendous impact on how you associate with people. Though you don't realize it, it is something that comes through in your body language. By being proactive and prepared, you will be confident, because you will be ready to handle most unexpected events. Confidence brings you so much respect from others and is a trait of charismatic people. When you are prepared, you will know you can handle most of the situations that are thrown your way, and it will show in the way you walk and talk. When you are prepared and proactive, you will have this level of confidence and therefore a better self-image.

Contingency Planning

Being proactive is a lot about planning. You have to plan for the known and anticipate the unknown to be proactive. This is called contingency planning. You are essentially planning for activities that might happen but have not happened yet. If all goes well, the activities might not happen at all and you would be in good shape. However, if you are prepared to handle the unexpected situations, then you do not have to worry about them. It is like the insurance policy that you take; the effort that you put in by preparing is like the premium that you pay for insurance. Contingency planning is about planning for things that could go wrong in your plan.

 Plans never go as planned. Be sure to account for contingencies.

How do you plan for contingencies? You need to concentrate on things that could go wrong. All of us have the tendency to think that we will achieve the goal without a problem. But when it comes to contingency planning, you forget about the goal and try to think of ways that would make it difficult to achieve it.

This is mainly a brainstorming exercise. Try to jot down all the ideas that you have, ranging from minor incidents to major incidents such as earthquakes. Once you have all your ideas down, try to short-list the ideas into the most probable things that could derail your goal and the ones that would have the worst impact on your goal.

The next step is to take each of those ideas and come up with alternative ways to stay on track. It is very important that you think through this process. If for some reason, there are things with a very high probability of happening, then do not only high-level planning, but also try to do detailed planning and gather the resources you would need.

Let's say you are studying for an exam while doing a job. You planned to study 15 hours a week at your desk for this exam. However, one of the very likely contingencies is that you could have a really big assignment at work that will drain you. When you come home, you would have no energy to study. What do you do?

You need a solution to this contingency as it is very likely that it could happen. One option would be to plan to take a day of vacation to catch up on studying; a second could be to plan to put the exam off to another day, if possible.

Similarly, you need to think of all the permutations that could derail you from your goal. It does not matter whether it is direct or indirect. If something could keep you from achieving your goal, you need to plan for it.

Contingency planning is all about being proactive. You prepare for the things that could go wrong. So when the unexpected happens, you know what to do. You can start to execute your contingency plans rather than figuring out how to tackle the situation.

Analyzing Your Competition

Most things in life entail competition. The resources in this world are limited. We can never have everything we want in life. Take your job. I am sure you would like to move up the ladder, get a promotion, or get a raise. There are always fewer positions than there are qualified people. Thus, you have competition.

A proactive person anticipates competition and plans for it. It is very similar to contingency planning. Your competition always tries to get ahead of you, as you would in their shoes. If you are not prepared for these situations, you lose out and will not have time to respond to most of these plans. A proactive person tries to predict these plans and prepares for them well in advance. When your competition makes a move, be prepared to get ahead of those moves.

Imagine for a moment that you are aiming for your boss's job. You know that your colleague is also interested in the same job. You have competition! The job requires you to be a trained manager. Your colleague might take a management course to better prepare him for this role. If he does, when the opportunity comes, he will be the best candidate. So, if you are aiming for the same job, you need to do the same now before he does and prepare for the next promotion. This is being proactive: anticipating the next move that your competition could take and preparing for it.

Let's not forget that, while we want to succeed, the rest of the world also wants to succeed. Though you don't want to look at life and career as a race, you still have to monitor your competition. Opportunities are scarce, and we have to compete for them. If there are any opportunities that are not drawing competition, they either soon will or they are not worth pursuing. This is the nature of things, and this is human behavior. We cannot go against human behavior, and we need to factor these in our road to success.

Having competition does not mean that we take a cutthroat approach to dealing with our competition. It is not correct to win at all costs. Everyone needs to win. When we win, we need to win keeping the long run in mind. Also, it does not mean that we give the world away to our competition. You need to succeed in the opportunities that are critical for your success. Life is a delicate balancing act, and there is no surefire formula to living life and succeeding. You need to know how to play it well.

There are also times when you need to think several steps ahead, not just about the immediate step. This is when you have competition that is also proactive. Most of the time, you will not have to deal with this situation. However, most high performers do respond quickly.

 Be ready for tomorrow.

To be proactive, you need to prepare for tomorrow today. I know the concept is simple and obvious, but most people generally don't follow this principle. In order to prepare for tomorrow, you need to know what will happen tomorrow. This is not an easy thing to do. Anybody can say what they think will happen tomorrow; knowing what truly will happen tomorrow is the difficult part. On your road to success, it is imperative that you have the ability to see what will happen in the next several years. It is certainly a guess, but it has to be an educated guess. You can always see the signs of tomorrow today.

As an example of how to read tomorrow today, let's look at tomorrow's technology and work trends. We know that cell phones are in everybody's hands and that people can do a lot of things with them.

(In fact, I used my phone sometimes to write sections of this book when I was waiting for the train.) At the same time, it is now a connected world. Almost every device is able to connect to the Internet without a single wire being connected. It is obvious based on these few trends that tomorrow's workforce needs to be mobile and will be accessible wherever they are. I don't foresee 9 to 5 workdays in the future, but I do see wireless handheld devices figuring prominently. If I'm to succeed tomorrow, I need to get familiar with cutting-edge mobile technology, not just that used to make calls, send e-mails, and listen to music (which is the norm today, by the way) but also to perform normal online functions such as banking. It means getting out of the comfort zone of your normal desktop or stack of papers and getting used to using small devices and being able to work anywhere. Although this is an obvious trend, try to understand some of the more subtle trends that are happening in your workplace and also around you.

Once you identify these trends, start preparing for them. Get used to trying new things and stepping out of your comfort zone. Take the cell phone example that I just gave: If you are used to working on a desktop computer with a nice big screen, you need to get used to doing your work on a screen one-tenth that size and typing on a lot smaller keyboard. Today's generation is already doing it. Give up what you already know to learn what you don't know. This will make you uncomfortable, and in the beginning you will struggle with some of the new change. However, it will make you prepared for what's to come. When change comes, you will be ready. Change is the only certainty in life.

Most of us change out of necessity. We are forced to change and adopt new ways. It is often not voluntary. In order for you to be successful, this change and learning needs to happen voluntarily. As easy as it is to say it, it is a lot more difficult to do. This is something I have to continuously remind myself as my comfort with what I know takes over. It is an uphill battle every day to make ourselves change, but this is what life calls us to do. In order for us to be successful, we need to learn to swim against the current.

Influencing Change

Another aspect of being proactive is influencing change. There are many times when you have to make change happen. You need to take things into your hands and give your goals a big push, because the goals are yours, not anyone else's. A lot of times, people expect the world and circumstances to fall in line so that they can achieve their goals. They blame their fate on the circumstances around them. If we are to be proactive, we need to start owning our fate and destiny and do what is necessary.

If you want something, you can't wait for it to come to you. Very few things in life will come to you while you wait. You need to move forward and get it.

Let's say you want to attend a training session, yet you are feeling shy to ask your manager. You are hoping that she will see your need and offer the training. Most likely, she will never realize it as she is busy doing her job. You need to make the move and ask for the training. We shouldn't wait without acting because we fear the worst. In most situations, the worst never happens, and we end up succeeding. All we need to do is simply step forward and influence the change.

Act before you're acted upon!

The world has its priorities. If your goal is a priority to you, make sure the world understands your priorities.

Realize that the world has its own priorities and wants. If you are to be successful, you must make sure your goals and aspirations get priority as well. This means influencing the change that you want. You have to take your goals and go out there to make your goals happen, despite the obstacles.

For example, if you want to have your manager's job and you are expecting that senior management will see you as a possible candidate, you are letting circumstances control your destiny. You need to be proactive and let your senior management know that you are interested when the position becomes open. You need to build your network of contacts and canvass the correct decision-makers so that when the opportunity comes, they think about you first. If you don't meet the requirements, at least you can work on meeting the requirements to do your manager's job. Being proactive means influencing the change you need by going out there.

Following up is another example of being proactive. The people who are in the places that can help you achieve your goals have their own priorities and agendas. When you ask for something and they agree to it, most of the time you need to follow up and put your request in front of them again.

One of my colleagues got approval for signing authority similar to a senior executive. This was the highest signing authority in an organization of 40,000 employees relative to their rank. Though nobody in the chain of command wanted to permit him this much authority, he got it through relentless follow-up and by being proactive. I have no doubt that he will continue to be very successful in his career. I know most of us would be worried about pestering top decision-makers, and at times his follow-up was borderline pestering, but it got the job done. I'm not asking you to pester people with your requests. The point I am trying to make is that you need to do what is necessary to influence the outcome you need. To be successful, this is required.

 There are people who ride the wave, and there are people who ride against the wave. To be successful, be someone who rides against the wave.

I believe there are two types of people when it comes to success: people who ride the wave and people who ride against the wave. People who ride the wave are successful when the circumstances are going in their direction. For example, when the market is doing well, these people make money, but when the market crashes, they drop like flies. They blame their fate on the market and wait for the next wave. Then there are people who ride against the wave. These people will do what needs to be done to get the job done. When the market is crashing, they will do whatever is required to ensure survival. Though they don't always get great results in tough times, when the market turns, the hard work that they did will start paying dividends. They work hard and influence the outcome. You need to be someone who will influence the outcome and do what needs to be done to ensure you meet your goals.

Conclusion

Being proactive is all about planning, planning, and planning. It is about anticipating the next move and being prepared for it. At the same time, being proactive should not be an excuse for inaction. Action needs to be taken always. You should be prepared to act, and also prepared for your competition.

CHAPTER 7

OVERCOMING FEAR

Fear keeps us from being our best.

W e all want to succeed. Nobody *wants* to be unsuccessful. But different things keep us away from the success that we want to achieve. I believe the answer lies within us. One fundamental factor that keeps us from being our best is fear. All of us live with some form of fear, to varying degrees and types. How we handle fear defines who we are. Our attitudes toward fear define how we take risks and how we perceive the world. Fear runs a lot deeper in us than we think. Most of us think that is merely physiological. In fact, fear is so embedded in our subconscious that most of the time we don't even know that is what is driving us.

Fear dampens our movement toward success. We need to overcome this fear.

Fear is a basic human instinct. We have developed this instinct to keep us away from danger and keep us safe. Most of the survival mechanisms our bodies relied on thousands of years ago are no longer relevant today, and yet the mechanisms are still there within us. Fear is one of those key mechanisms. We need to consciously overcome it.

For us to succeed in our careers and life, we need to understand what we fear. It comes in all shapes and sizes. One common trait of all forms of fear is that it dampens our movement toward success.

Each of us has a fear profile. We develop this profile as we grow up and experience things in life. Our attitudes toward fear and risk change with our experiences. However, how we react to certain events in our past depends on the individual. For example, 9/11 made certain people more fearful while it made others fearless. One thing is for certain: 9/11 changed all of us. It changed our whole outlook on the evils of terrorism.

You become confident by learning to fly in the face of fear.

People who succeed are not the ones without fear. They have fears also. But they have made the choice to overcome fear. Once you overcome it, you become confident and realize that there was nothing to fear in the first place.

Fear is a subconscious inhibitor of our movement toward success. The difficulty lies in overcoming a subconscious feeling consciously. To suppress fear is a choice that we make. Knowing that it is there within us, we decide to move against it. This is why I mentioned that the choices that we make define us.

Coming back to my original point, if you really think about it, there is no one who does not want to be successful. The need to succeed is within us, and we are all born with it. Yet something keeps us away from it. Some manage to be successful anyway, but most cannot. This is fear. To identify what we fear, we have to be truthful to ourselves and search deep within us to understand it. Because fear is such an important aspect in your road to success, I want to dedicate this chapter to a detailed discussion of fear and how to overcome it.

What Is Fear?

This is an important question. If we fully understood it, humanity wouldn't have half the problems it has today. What we do know about fear is that it is a basic instinct and it helps us keep away from danger. From a survival perspective, it is an important part of being human.

However, this instinct is one of the basic reasons that we cannot achieve our potential and be successful.

We need to deal with factors, like fear, that inhibit our success.

Very few books about success talk about its core inhibitors. Fear is one of those core inhibitors. It slows us down and keeps us from being our best. In the modern human being, it is actually a flaw. You learned to be fearful before you could even talk, and it is a skill that we all learn extremely fast.

You cannot overcome fear—you must choose to go against it.

You cannot live in a world without fear. Nor is there a pill that you can take to overcome it. There are no techniques to drive your fears away. This is one of the basic human instincts that has been there from the time we were born. There is only one thing we can do about fear—choose to go against it.

Forms of Fear

Most of the reasons we give for why we can't be our best are based on a fear. Most forms of fear cannot be easily identified. They all run deep within us and need to be sought within us in order to be identified. Of the many forms of fear, the following are common:

- Fear of change
- Fear of perfection
- Fear of the unknown
- Fear of confrontation

You might think to yourself that you don't have any of these. However, deep down, it's possible you have one of these fears. I've always searched for the reason why I procrastinate. I never thought that it might relate to fear. Recently, I realized that it was in fact due to fear of perfection. Since then, I've been able to overcome procrastination very easily. Only you know whether you are fearful. You need to be truthful to yourself.

Let's look at some of these fears in detail:

Fear of change: This is a common reason why most of us don't adapt well to new changes. It's not that we don't want to change as we get older; rather, we get comfortable with what we know. Learning something new means risking what we know. New knowledge might not be as good as what we already know. Learning something new also means putting extra effort into learning. If you have this fear, acknowledge it. Know that your fear of change might turn out to be unfounded, and make the choice to learn something new.

Fear of perfection: This is another common form of fear where we don't do anything because we fear that our efforts would not yield a perfect result. It is in fact the fear of making a mistake. We fear that if we are to do anything, we will make a mistake and the end result will not live up to our standards. If you face this fear, you need to understand that you are human. To be human is to be imperfect. Everything in this world has flaws. It is in fact this imperfection that makes society possible. We lean on each other to capitalize on our strengths because we all have weaknesses.

It is ironic that we view society as perfect. Everything will not be perfect on the first go. We have to realize that making a mistake is all right. One approach I take to overcome this fear is to lower my standards on my first attempt doing something, like writing a chapter. I then go back and correct my mistakes. I used to think that I couldn't write because I wouldn't be able to come up with the perfect chapter. I grew out of this fear and realized that nothing is perfect. Once I overcame this fear, words started to flow, and I realized that I do a pretty good job after I have the first draft.

Fear of the unknown: Another common fear is that of what we don't know. This is very similar to the fear of change. It is a form of laziness to be comfortable with what we know. It is easy to comfortable. We fear that the unknown could not be as good as what we know. We forget that when we learned what we know today, we actually had to overcome the same fear to start off with; otherwise, we wouldn't know what we know. We get comfortable with the little that we know, and we gain comfort. For us to be human is to venture into the unknown. It is people who have ventured into the unknown that made society possible. Every day, we have to go to the unknown. Yes we will make mistakes. Yet there is a world of possibilities, and we need to explore them. We can't hide behind fear of making a few mistakes.

Fear of confrontation: We become shy and don't want to confront people or difficult situations. Whether introvert or extrovert, all of us have this fear. We fear confrontation because we worry about not being able to say the right things or coming across properly. What we don't realize is that the other person whom we're talking to feels the same. Though we all make mistakes in conversation, most of our conversations do not go badly. In difficult situations, if you prepare well, you could avoid even the few mistakes you might make.

 Fear hides deep within us. We need to be truthful to ourselves and search within us to find what we fear.

We need to search within ourselves and identify what is keeping us from success, and confronting fear is another aspect to work on in cultivating success. It is also important to work on what is slowing you down. There are numerous books out there about time management and effectiveness. These books outline a number of fabulous techniques and principles on being effective and successful. One thing that is not adequately addressed in most of this literature is overcoming your fears. It is great to make lists, prioritize tasks, schedule activities, and have all the right tools. But if we are fearful of our tasks and our fear is keeping us away from achieving these tasks, these plans are not going anywhere.

Before we discuss how to overcome fear, let's discuss some of the real-world situations that are caused by fear:

Procrastination: While we procrastinate for a number of reasons, most of the time, the real reason behind our procrastination is fear. We can schedule our activities and our time, but in order to execute on these activities, we have to make ourselves stick to these plans, which is the most difficult part. Most of the time, the answer lies not in the system but within ourselves. Given that we know our priorities and we know how to do it, there must be something within ourselves that is keeping us from executing these plans. We need to identify what that is. Once you identify it, it is easy to address.

Keeping us from career opportunities: Again, on your road to success in your career, it makes logical sense for you to go to the next level. You might have the right skills, yet you hesitate. It could be that you fear additional responsibility and that you think you might not be able to do a great job. If you are faced with this situation, you need to understand that in every job there is a learning curve and you will learn your new job. If you were forced into that role, you would learn it, so why not give it a chance now?

Family issues: A lot of family issues are also caused by fear; most of the time our primary problem is fear of confrontation: not being able to say what you really have to say because you fear that it will be taken the wrong way. So we wait until things get out of control. We are then forced to confront the situation. If you can put your fears aside and put all the points on the table with your spouse from the outset, there are a lot of things you can resolve.

Though the solutions to most of our problems are clear and logical, it is our emotional selves that keep us away from these solutions. It is our emotional selves that we need to resolve first before we start resolving a problem or going after a goal. You need to succeed first within yourself before you can with others. You need to win the battle over your emotions.

Courage and Success

To be successful, we need to be courageous. To be courageous means to overcome our fears. Even in our simple day-to-day tasks, there is a certain level of courage that is required. The only way to overcome your fear is to move against it. Once you move against it, you will realize that, most of the time, your fears are baseless.

Contrary to popular thinking, high performers are not people who have special abilities and skills. They just make correct choices and move against their fears. One common trait that they all have is that they understand their fears, face them, and make the choice to move against them.

Learning to manage your fears is a sign of becoming a leader.

In fact, the higher you go up the corporate ladder, the less technical you get. You start developing leadership traits. One of the basic leadership traits is having courage. To succeed in your career and your life, you have to be courageous. Courage is simply the choice you make to move against your fear. The higher you go up the corporate ladder, the lonelier it is. You have to take responsibility for your decisions and actions. Sometimes, it means taking responsibility for your mistakes. There are many fears that leaders have, far more than when they started their careers, because they have less of a support system. However, they make the choice to move on in the face of this fear. This is what you call leadership and courage. That is why people look up to them. This ability is a learned ability. You start small, and over time you overcome your fears and become confident. That is why the way we handle fear defines who we are.

Conclusion

On your road to success, you need to move against your fear. You might know all the steps to your ultimate goal, but if you choose not to go against your fears, then you will not move forward. Make the choice to move against your fear. Be courageous. You can do anything if you choose to do it. It is your choices that will define you.

CHAPTER 8

BELIEVE IN YOURSELF

The lives that we have are tremendously valuable. We instinctively know it, which is why survival is the most basic human need. However, at a conscious level, we sometimes do not value ourselves as we should. We let others ride our lives and use us. Because we do not value ourselves, we rarely believe in ourselves.

 We need to value ourselves based on what we think of ourselves rather than what others think of us.

To be successful, we need to believe in ourselves and value ourselves. We need to value ourselves based on what we think rather than what others think. How we value ourselves and to what extent we believe in ourselves have tremendous implications on our success. Our entire confidence is based on how we value ourselves.

Most important, how we overcome our fears is solely dependent on what we think of ourselves. We cannot change our perception of ourselves overnight. Our perception of ourselves largely comes from our upbringing. We can certainly change it if we want. It takes searching within us to identify how we value ourselves. Once you know what drives this value within you, then you can change your perception of yourself and start believing in yourself. It might feel artificial to think differently of yourself at first, but as time goes on, your perceptions will change.

Valuing yourself based on what you think doesn't mean ignoring the rest of the world and your relationships. Our success depends on the interactions that we have with the rest of the world. We do need to adjust ourselves based on the feedback that we get from the rest of society.

Like anything else in life, this is a constant process of balancing. Balancing requires us to be aware of both sides of the equation and not go on "autopilot." We have to be thinking constantly. Thinking requires us to put effort into every moment of our lives. That is what life is all about. The more effort we put in, the more we get out of life. In this chapter, I would like to talk in detail about valuing and believing in ourselves as it is very important to our success.

The Need to Value Ourselves

We need to value ourselves and believe in ourselves before we start doing the same for others. This is why in most relationships, whether they are business or personal, it is very difficult to have a healthy relationship with someone who does not value himself or herself. Though you might think of it as selfless dedication, it is a burden for the other person. It appears that you are expecting constant recognition from the other person. For him or her, you become a burden. Relationships are important in our lives. It is important that we have healthy relationships based on our individuality both at work and in our personal lives.

Healthy relationships depend on how we value ourselves.

Healthy relationships happen between two independent people. When we are dependent on each other, the relationship is based not on choice but on dependency and benefit. Though initially it might seem healthy, the relationship becomes problematic because the independent person starts feeling used. In many marriages, this is the situation. I knew of a family where the wife was unwilling to drive. She associated this inability to drive with a fender-bender that happened years ago. From what I could see, the accident was merely an excuse for her to become dependent on her spouse. At times, the husband felt that there was an undue burden on him because his wife was unable to do anything without him. He felt that he was an accessory rather than a partner in their relationship. Even in business, a situation where an employee is dependent on the manager for guidance, support, and recognition, the employee's prospects of getting promoted are hindered when it appears that the employee is unable to take responsibility and be independent.

It is when we value ourselves that we become independent. We judge ourselves and feel adequate based on the value we place on ourselves. If we do not value ourselves, we are forced to obtain that value through someone else. This is when we become dependent. What does valuing ourselves have to do with believing in ourselves? We need to value ourselves before we can believe in ourselves. If we do not value who we are, there is little that we can believe. To believe in ourselves is to have faith in our abilities and to trust our judgment. If we do not value our judgment, then we cannot believe in it. We believe in people when we see value in them.

Once we can value ourselves, we can begin to value others. This is key, because on our road to success and relationships, we need to start seeing the value that others bring to the table and be able to capitalize on this value. We create a tremendous bond when we value the other person in a relationship. Both parties in the relationship feel valued. This is crucial for your success, because you succeed through others. In order to learn to value others, we need to learn to value ourselves first. We perceive the world differently. If the perception that we have of ourselves is lack of value, then our perception of others is most likely the same.

I once had a boss who did not value himself. It was evident through our day-to-day interaction because he perceived his team the same way. We (the team) were no more than a commodity for him rather than actual people with opinions. If he valued us as people, then he would have realized we were more than paid resources and that we had valuable opinions. The team would have been a lot more productive because of the ideas each individual contributor offered. In this case these ideas were not valued. This shows the value our leaders/managers place on themselves tremendously effects the productivity of the group they lead.

Feeling Adequate

The value that we put on ourselves affects our feeling of adequacy. This is why I felt it was important to talk about the value that we place on ourselves. Feeling adequate is very important because our confidence depends on it. Feeling adequate is how we view ourselves relative to the world. It is that feeling that tells us, "I'm okay." As simple as it sounds, many people do not have this feeling. I have seen this trait only in high performers, which leads me to believe that it is something that differentiates success from failure. We often see people who surround themselves with different things—electronic accessories, expensive cars, and much else. Some people surround themselves with these material things to feel adequate.

In order to overcome our fears, we need to feel adequate. In Chapter 7, I talked about how fear affects the road to success. In order to overcome fear, we also need to feel secure and feel adequate. We cannot overcome our fears if we think that we are not ready and adequate to take on the new things in our lives.

Our confidence lies on how adequate we feel. If we do not feel that we are adequate for the task, we do not have the confidence to move forward. For example, say you are preparing a report to send to senior management. If you do not feel that you have adequately done the necessary diligence, you would be analyzing the data or proofreading it without sending the report to senior management. Until you feel that you are "okay," you probably won't feel comfortable doing anything. Therefore, feelings of adequacy are important for you to move forward with confidence.

The Benefits of Valuing Yourself

The value that we place on ourselves has a tremendous impact on a number of factors for success.

As mentioned earlier, valuing yourself and believing in yourself is important and can influence your road to success. Many aspects that influence success depend on it. Let's look at some of these influences.

Confidence

Your confidence is a direct result of how you value yourself and your feelings of adequacy. It is obvious that success is a direct result of the level of confidence you have. If you are good at gauging people's level of confidence, you will realize that there is a significant difference in employees' confidence at each level of the hierarchy.

One of my managers once told me, "If you need to get to the next level, you need to act as if you are in the next level." I see the value in this statement now because he was talking about the level of confidence you need to have in what you are doing. We all want better pay and opportunities. All of us want the promotion. Promotions generally come to employees who have that level of confidence for their next role in their current role.

You can't fake confidence. People who are confident and have to make tough decisions can easily tell the difference between real confidence and fake confidence. You can surround yourself with gadgets, nice clothes, and smooth talking to vouch for your confidence. Nevertheless, on a day-to-day basis, it is difficult to keep this up. Your real level of confidence eventually shows through. To really be confident, you need to address the drivers of your confidence, which are:

- Value that you place on yourself
- Your feelings of adequacy
- Your faith in yourself

Your true confidence is a result of these core drivers. Once you develop your core drivers, you will have the confidence you require. Your level of confidence is vital for your success. I cannot stress this fact more. For you to move up the corporate ladder and succeed in life, you have to build your confidence.

Overcoming Fear

As mentioned before, our feelings of adequacy determine how we face fear and how courageous we are. Everyone has fear. It is a basic instinct, and it is normal. To be courageous means to fly in the face of fear. It is a choice that we make, and for us to be successful, we need to be courageous every day.

It would be difficult to make that choice if we did not feel adequate. We cannot justify the choice if we don't consider ourselves valuable. Only if we consider ourselves more valuable than the challenge at hand can we make the choice to move forward in the face of fear. It is human nature to go with the most valuable.

Even in nature, things flow from high to low, such as water that flows from a high place to a low place. We act the same way. We act on what we perceive as high value. If we consider ourselves of a lower value, then we will never overcome challenges and never make the choice to move forward. It is imperative that you start valuing yourself, knowing this.

For example, I came from a third-world country. The decision to immigrate to another country when everything was fine for me in my home country was difficult. Having done it once, I knew I would have a number of challenges, and naturally, I feared it. However, I made the decision to move my family here because I valued myself. I knew that I deserved a better life. Knowing that enabled me to overcome these fears that I had, face the challenges, give up everything I had, and start all over again. If I had not valued myself, I would not have been able to make that choice.

Similarly, when you value yourself, you can overcome your fears because you perceive yourself as greater than the challenges in front of you. It is obvious that this trait is very important to be successful.

Self-Preservation and Fulfillment of Purpose

As discussed in Chapter 1, one of our primary purposes in life is to enjoy the life that we have. Life is a privilege, despite the problems that we might have. We know it instinctively, which is why we all try to survive rather than give up quickly.

By valuing ourselves, we preserve our identity and contribute toward our primary reason for living. When we value ourselves, we can start growing. We cannot grow until we believe that our life means something.

Respect in Society

Though we discussed what we gain by valuing ourselves, let us also look at what would happen if we should continue on a path of not valuing and not believing in ourselves.

We gain respect from society for various reasons. Well-respected people generally gain respect for their achievements and knowledge. However, if we fail to value ourselves, we would not gain respect but would lose respect. Our self-worth does not come out openly; it comes out through our actions and our behavior. The way we interact with people and our choices depend on our self-worth. If our self-worth is less than optimal, society will see this. Though we would not gain more respect than any other person just for having self-worth, we would certainly lose respect in society if we did not have self-worth. This would hinder your drive toward success because others would see your ideas and actions in a different light.

For example, imagine that you are a person who always accommodates other people's requests at work. You now need to go on vacation, but your vacation falls during a busy time. When you request time off, your manager tells you immediately that you cannot take that time away. However, your colleague who works in a similar role gets his vacation time approved, and you end up covering for your colleague as well.

When you do not have respect, you probably feel that people step on you and use you for their own reasons. You actually feel that people steal from you to accomplish their agendas. The reason that this is happening and that you are feeling this way is because you let this happen. If you do not value yourself, other people's requests hold greater value than your own. You send the signal to the world that you are not valuable. Others are happy to take advantage of your gift. Very rarely will you get any recognition for it.

Credibility

 There are three types of credibility. The most fundamental—personality-based credibility—depends on our self-worth.

Credibility is again crucial to our success. It is something that we gain over time based on who we are and what we accomplish in life. We need to build our credibility in order to become successful. To succeed in life and in our careers, we need to win the hearts and minds of people around us. We do that through our credibility. There are three forms of credibility:

1. **Positional:** Based on our role in an organization, positional credibility comes automatically. For example, when a new senior executive joins an organization, what he or she says has a certain level of credibility even though employees do not know him.

2. **Experience-based:** Based on what we have achieved in our past, we gain this level of credibility. For example, if you have delivered three major projects successfully, you will have gained the credibility as a great project manager. The comments you provide on other projects have great impact.

3. **Personality-based:** This credibility comes through our personality. It largely comes through how we speak, how we interact, and how we appear. Our self-worth is a large determinant of all these factors that make up personality-based credibility. If we do not have personality-based credibility, then the other two forms of credibility make little difference.

Our personality-based credibility is the core form of credibility that the other two forms rest on. We might get a great job as a senior manager, but if our personality-based credibility is lacking, we will lose the positional and experience-based credibility as well.

Personality-based credibility is largely a result of our self-worth and valuing ourselves. When we value ourselves, we keep promises to ourselves. Because we are able to self-manage and keep promises to ourselves, we are better suited to keep promises to other people, thereby affecting our personality-based credibility. In addition, when we have self-worth, the tone when we talk is very different from the way someone without self-worth talks. We come out as confident and sure of ourselves. Again, this adds to our personality-based credibility. Your charisma depends on your personality-based credibility.

High performers have charisma and high levels of personality-based credibility. When they say something, everyone knows that what they say is true and many people believe them. In many presidential races, this trait wins people's hearts and minds.

Because you have self-worth, you can be decisive. Again, this is a trait that high performers have. They are people who are quick to make a decision. This is because they know where they are in terms of their principles. They place new information in their perceptual map very quickly because they value themselves and know who they are. They do not spend time evaluating trivial decisions for too long.

Thus, credibility is very important to your success. You build your credibility by valuing yourself and developing your self-worth. In the next section, let us look at how to develop your self-worth. Even if you think you value yourself correctly, this is an area in which all of us can improve.

How Do You Value Yourself?

You can change your self-worth for the better.

Again, building your self-worth largely depends on your choices and desires. You own your destiny. No matter what your past is, your future depends on the choices that you make today. In order to build your self-worth and start valuing yourself, you can take action.

You need to keep several things in mind.

Know Your Achievements

No matter how small they are, you need to start recognizing your achievements. I dedicated Chapter 16 to this, as it is important to know your achievements to build your self-worth. No matter where you are in the organization or in life, you have done things that will make you proud. Quite often, we rarely recognize these achievements. In order to build your self-worth, you need to identify these and recognize them consciously.

Whenever, I draft my resume, I get a huge confidence boost. It is only then I realize what I have done to this point. On a day-to-day basis, we are involved in so many urgent and critical efforts, such as raising our children, that we hardly stop to recognize what we have done. Quite often, you need to stop and recognize your achievements. As I discuss in Chapter 16, you need to list them as if you are trying to draft your resume. Once you do that, step back and realize what you have done in the big picture.

When you know your achievements, you will start realizing that you are far better equipped to handle many situations than you originally thought.

Be Realistic

Be realistic about yourself. You need to realize that despite the issues you might have had, you have achieved quite a lot. You might have not achieved your entire goal, but you have achieved 75 percent of it. If you are disappointed about not achieving the rest of your goal, you are not valuing yourself. Instead look at the 75 percent you have achieved, which is 75 percent more than you would have if you hadn't started at all.

For example, for a long time, I was trying to lose excess weight that I had gained over the past ten years. I wanted to lose 40 pounds by the end of the year, as this would get me to my ideal weight. This year I started my quest. It is now December, and I have managed to lose 30 pounds. I have not achieved my goal, but if I consider the other things that were going on in my life, I have done quite well. From a realistic perspective, I have achieved quite a lot.

At the same time, though you cannot become the CEO next year, you still might be able to obtain a promotion to the next level or even find a new job next year. Set realistic goals that you can achieve within your timeframe. Do not forget that life will throw difficult challenges at you, but if you set realistic goals, you will get good, achievable results—and protect your self-worth in the process. It is important to make realistic promises to ourselves. When we don't, we damage our self-worth unnecessarily.

Strategize, Strategize, Strategize

Do not just make promises to yourself. You need to strategize your goals and act on them. Strategy is a key component of our success. If we do not act on our goals, it is the same as breaking promises to ourselves. Our self-worth gets hurt.

Once you decide to do something, you need to use strategy to achieve it. Use the strategy tool to not only plan it but also execute it. The self-worth that you gain by achieving your own goals is tremendous. These are not like achieving someone else's goal, such as increasing profitability for the company. These are your goals and your results.

The weight that I lost gave me a tremendous confidence boost, not simply because I look better but also because I have managed to work hard and do something for myself. It has made me think of myself as someone who could get something done.

If you have problems keeping promises to yourself, you can start by getting small things done. Again, be realistic about what you can do. If you have missed your goals consistently, it could be that you are overplanning. Set small goals by using strategy. Then you can move on to bigger projects and challenges.

Overcome Your Fears

Recognize your achievements and start realizing that you are a lot better than what you thought you were. Based on this, you can make the choice to move forward despite the fears that you have. I talked about how you can go about this in Chapter 7.

Stand Up for What You Believe

No one will stand up for what you believe other than you. If you think that something is wrong, work to correct it. Stand behind your principles, and do not let the world talk you into another mindset. If you do not stand up for what you believe, the world will walk all over you. You will feel strained and let down.

You will feel a lot more confident being the only one standing for yourself than agreeing with someone else simply because it's easier. If this requires you to take drastic action such as looking for another job, then you can strategize how to do it and execute it.

When I was living in my previous country, the corruption and the unfairness of life was against what I believed. I could do nothing about it. It was widespread. It had become part of the culture of that country. While the country had many great things, this aspect was against what I believed. I decided to leave the country and start all over again because I wanted to stand up for what I believed. As a result, I have gained far more confidence in myself to do the right thing.

Conclusion

Value yourself. Your self-worth has a tremendous impact on your success. Your confidence and your life depend on how you value yourself. No matter what your past is, you can influence your self-worth by doing things in line with what you believe.

CHAPTER 9

BEING PASSIONATE
ABOUT YOUR GOALS

It is passion that gives us the energy to go after things. Passion is an invisible force that drives us toward success. Passion drives people to be great and do things beyond their imagination. You don't have to have talent to be successful; you need passion. You can do anything, anything at all, only if you have the passion. So, what does it mean to be passionate? It is in fact a number of factors coming together to form a tremendous force that drives you. The best part is that it is something you can develop. Passion is a set of skills that you acquire and cultivate.

Why Should You Be Passionate?

Being passionate gives you energy and drive on your road to success.

Being passionate and caring about your goals gives you a tremendous amount of energy and drive. It motivates you to achieve and give the best even in the hardest times when all else fails. Passion keeps you going.

In every plan and every goal in life, you are going to face challenging times. Once the initial hype wears off, there will be a time in every journey and every plan when it becomes mundane. Passion will take you through this period. Whether it is losing weight, saving for a vacation, or inventing the next big thing, all of us face challenges in our journey to success. If we are passionate about what we are doing, we will overcome all these challenges.

Wanting to achieve a goal and actually working to achieve it are two different things. Working on your goals can be very difficult at times. There are times when you have to remind yourself why you are doing what you are doing. Being passionate will take you through to the end.

High performers are rarely high performers by birth. If that were the case, the A students in high school would always do well in life. In reality, we know this is not the case. While talent helps, it is not a prerequisite for success. You don't have to have talent to achieve a goal. If you have the passion, you will have the drive to take you toward success.

None of my family members were accountants, nor did I have any accounting background. I disliked accounting in my school days. Yet I wanted to be an accountant late in my career, and I developed a passion for it. I was able to start in the accounting profession with basic courses, go on to become a certified accountant, and work as a senior finance manager. How did I get there without having any talent or background in accounting? I was very passionate about achieving my goal of being an accountant. Passion kept me going. In fact, there were times that I thought to myself, "Why am I doing this?" Passion lets you achieve tremendous things. I believe it is the main element of success. It allows you to summon resources and be good at the things that you are not. It is the prime motivator.

Passion is the lifeblood of success. Without passion, the plans that you make would be useless. Passion gives you the energy to move forward and takes you through the ups and downs of your plans. The relationship between success and passion is very strong. You cannot have success without passion. In order to achieve your goals, you need to have the desire and passion to achieve those goals. All of us have goals and aspirations, but it is people who have passion that achieve them. This is why success is closely related to how passionate we are.

I consider myself to be an average person coming from an average background. When I was growing up, I wasn't a straight-A student, nor did I fail all my studies. When I started working, I wasn't an overperformer. In fact, I would have placed myself below average because I was new to the culture and didn't understand the cultural forces. Nor did I have great networks or resources. However, one thing I knew I had was the passion to become successful. I saw high performers and wanted to be like them. I always wanted to do well in life, like anybody else. Not only did I want to have it, I had a passion to achieve it. This passion gave me drive to look at myself and improve almost every aspect of myself to become a high performer like others.

This is why I say that passion is the only thing you need to start with. If you have resources to springboard yourself to success, then you have an edge. However, if you don't, you need only passion to become successful. Passion drives us to great heights and gives us the energy to do things that we never thought we could do.

When you are passionate, opportunities open up for you.

People see our passion in the way we work. It opens wonderful opportunities. I recall two colleagues I knew during the financial meltdown of 2008. One had better academic qualifications and more experience than the other, but he also saw his job as a daily chore. Though he was a decent worker, he didn't have passion for his work. He did what needed to be done. The other colleague did whatever was needed to get the job done. He was more service-oriented and a lot more passionate. When the time came for cutbacks, to everyone's surprise, the more qualified colleague lost his job and the more passionate colleague took over his work. Purely from a skills perspective, I think they were both the same. But from a soft trait perspective, they were different. The one who was more passionate was clearly more productive.

People see your level of passion through your work and how you behave. Though nobody could put a finger on who has more passion, I think instinctively we know. If I were a manager, I would choose the person who had more passion in an interview. It is the passionate person who will get things done and live through difficult times to achieve their goals. If you are to succeed in life, you need to develop your passion. It is something that all of us can attain if we want to.

So what are the elements of passion, and how do you develop them?

Developing a Passion for Goals

If you try to break down passion into its individual components, you will realize that passion is made out of things that are completely within our control. It is possible to be consciously passionate about things, and it is also possible to develop this passion.

If you break down passion into its components, you get the following:

- Taking ownership
- Being disciplined
- Being focused
- Being committed
- Having faith

Let's look at each of these factors one by one and explore how you can develop each.

Taking Ownership

 It is important to take ownership of your goals and destiny.

Taking ownership is one of the important factors of passion. You are responsible for your destiny and your goals. To be passionate about something, you need to own the task at hand and take responsibility. If you don't own the task, it is extremely difficult to have feelings for it. It is human nature not to love something you don't own. Passion is a form of love for what you do.

With anything in life, we need to have ownership to develop a passion. Some form of ownership is necessary to have commitment. In relationships, though we don't want to say it, we seek ownership of the other person. If not, you would not get hurt if the other person left you. Though we deny ownership of a person all out, if you examine any relationship, where there is love, this is a form of ownership and bonding. This is because in order for us to love someone or something, we need to know that it will be ours. Without ownership, love is almost impossible.

The same is true for your goals and plans. For you to be passionate and love what you do, you need to have ownership of the task. Take, for instance, your job: You will not be able to do well without being passionate about the work you do. To be passionate, you need to take ownership of the task. However, most people don't take ownership because it is not their own company. To take ownership, you don't need to physically own the company. You don't need to have legal ownership. Taking ownership is a sense of belonging to the task and also caring for the task. You take a personal interest in the task. This personal interest is what forms part of the passion you have toward the task.

So, for your goals and plans, tell yourself that they are yours. Not only should you tell yourself, but also believe it in your heart. It makes a big difference. During difficult times, fight for your goals; they are your goals. Constantly remind yourself that the goals are yours. You'll be amazed by the energy that you generate, and also by the results. Take care of your goals.

Being Disciplined

Discipline is interrelated with all the other factors that form passion. It comes through having focus.

Discipline is delaying your rewards to a later time and working hard now to achieve your goals.

Genuinely, most of us don't have much discipline. It's our human nature. This is why all the bright ideas we get on a daily basis hardly get executed. Discipline is essentially sticking to your plans and enjoying the benefits later. We also call this persistence—sticking with your goal through thick and thin. It is being married to your goals and working at them not only during times of excitement but also when it is extremely difficult and mundane. You need to persevere to discipline yourself. You need to constantly remind yourself why you are doing what you are doing.

Execute the tasks at any cost. When I say cost, I mean at the expense of personal pleasures. It is the daily pleasures such as relaxing or watching TV that keep us away from our goals most of the time. To discipline yourself, always remind yourself of your goal, and always work on your goal.

You need to discipline yourself to achieve your goals. It is one of the factors that make up passion. Discipline will keep you focused on the target goal.

Life will always throw various opportunities at you. Notice I am not calling them obstacles because you, as an intelligent person, would know how to avoid obstacles. It is the opportunities that we have problems with. The good keeps us away from the best. We as humans have limited time and energy. If we took advantage of all the choices and opportunities we encountered, we wouldn't be able to succeed at anything. High performers are people who choose their opportunities and do well with the opportunities they choose.

Even from an emotional standpoint, there will always be situations when doing something different will satisfy you emotionally. Let's say you have a goal of losing weight, but when you come home you are hungry and you crave a nice hamburger. Would you rather stick to your goal or satisfy your emotional need by having the hamburger? I know it is a very difficult choice! Having discipline will keep you focused on your goals. You need to keep your eye on your goals no matter what opportunities come your way.

To discipline yourself, when you get a tempting opportunity, remember to ask yourself how the opportunity will affect your goal. Will it delay achieving your goal? Will it cause you to abandon your goal? Will the opportunity enhance it or will it destroy it? If it helps your goal, then you need to take the opportunity. You need to evaluate each of these factors to determine how the opportunity will help your goal.

What happens in situations where you know that the opportunity is not good for your goal, yet you decide to take it? You know you are doing something wrong, yet you continue doing it. You need to try to work hard in this situation. You need to break away from the temptation. If an addiction is keeping you away from a goal, you actually need to temporarily put your goal on hold and make it your goal to deal with the addiction. Addictions are not necessarily just smoking or alcohol. It could be a specific thing like starchy foods or watching too much TV. Breaking away from your addiction is a major effort. You need to overcome your addiction before you think about your goal. Overcoming your addiction should be your intermediate goal.

For instance, say the hunger you have at the end of the day keeps you from losing weight. No matter what you do, you simply cannot give up the craving when it comes, even though you know it is the wrong thing. You lose weight in the short run, but you keep on bouncing back because of your craving. You have a problem. You are addicted to the craving. You need to strategize and resolve the issue before you think about losing weight.

If you have discipline issues, address them first. You need to be disciplined to achieve your goals. It is a key component of being passionate.

Being Focused

You need to be focused and divert your energy toward your goal.

Focus diverts all your energy to the task or the goal. Without focus, a lot of things would not be possible. People who focus on the task at hand are the ones who finally achieve the task. Without focus, it is impossible to achieve. Through choice we bring about focus.

On your journey to any goal, there are difficult times, and there are times when things are very easy. It is during difficult times that we give up most of our goals. Being focused gets us out of this dilemma. It keeps all the energy focused on the task at hand.

Discipline and taking ownership are ways of being focused on your task. Being focused is a key factor in being passionate. Often focus comes from self-directing ourselves. When we tell ourselves to focus, we focus. Surprisingly, we obey our own words and our own internal thoughts. It sometimes feels that there are two different people living within us—one who is logical and one who is emotional. When

I have days when I simply cannot focus, I use this technique to gain control of myself.

When I initially read about it, I didn't believe it. However, the first time I tried it, it was very effective. It seems that I listen well to my own words and direction. We have an internal voice that we listen to, and we can use it to bring focus to our lives. It is a guiding mentor to tell us what to do.

We need to learn to use this voice to direct ourselves. When we were young, there were people to tell us what to do, like our parents and teachers. As we grew older and became mature, we no longer had anybody telling us what to do. That's when we must begin using our inner voice to direct ourselves.

To succeed, we need to divert all our energy away from the day-to-day distractions and focus on our priorities.

To succeed, focus is very important. Most of us are distracted by the everyday urgencies of life such as children, shopping, and our job. We have to learn to prioritize what we need to achieve and bring focus to our priorities. All of us know how to prioritize. We know that our goals are important. There are many books written on how to prioritize. But what most of us don't do is focus on our priorities and execute them. To succeed, you have to do both.

I have met colleagues who can focus but cannot prioritize. They are able to work long hours and keep going, which I admire. Unfortunately, they seem to be spinning their wheels. At the same time, there are people who know what is important but can't get it done. They have so many other urgencies in life. Focus brings our priorities into action.

Being focused means keeping away from distractions and deviations. All deviations and distractions from your goal need to be individually evaluated. If it adversely affects your goal, then you need to keep away from the distraction.

Being Committed

Staying focused and being committed are also interrelated. You need a full commitment to your goal. Dedication to what you are doing is very important. Being committed not only keeps you focused but also helps you direct all your energy toward your goal or your plan. You need high levels of energy to be a high performer. No matter what your physical state is, you'll get this energy through your commitment and passion. You need every ounce of energy to take you through the difficult times.

Being passionate means being committed. Most of us think that commitment comes from being passionate, but I think it is different. *Passion is a product of your commitment.* Commitment is something that is controllable and achievable. Passion comes out of the commitment that you have to the task. You can tell yourself to be committed, which will make you passionate about your goal. However, telling yourself to be passionate does not necessarily make you committed.

Commitment is a promise that you make to yourself.

To be committed, you need to make a vow to yourself that you will achieve your goal. You need to tell yourself, "I am committed to achieving this goal." Not only is it necessary that you make a vow, but you also need to respect your vow because you are making a promise to yourself. You are valuable. You need to respect yourself and keep to this commitment. Once you make a commitment to yourself, you have to keep it. If you go back on it, you are destroying your sense of value to yourself. You will undoubtedly lose self-confidence. Though you don't realize it, it will happen. It will affect all your goals. So if you are going to make a commitment, make sure that the goal you are going to achieve is absolutely your final choice and decision. Once you make this commitment, keep to this commitment at all costs.

Making a commitment to yourself is not like making a commitment to someone else. If you keep your commitment, then you will gain self-confidence. However, if you break your commitment, you are going to lose self-confidence. Unlike most things in life, there is nothing in the middle. It is far more important than keeping commitments to other people.

Having Faith

Believe in yourself to achieve your goal.

Finally, you need to believe in yourself and your goal. You can do anything if you put your mind to it. The reason you have set a goal is because you can achieve it. You are valuable, and the goal is valuable to you. Believe that you can do it, and be confident that you can achieve it. Setting a goal and strategizing is going to be worthless if you don't believe in yourself, the goal, and your own intrinsic value. Without that faith, the work that you are doing is going to be just mechanical, and the end result that you achieve will not be the perfect result. So believe in yourself that you can achieve the goal.

You constantly need to tell yourself that you can achieve the goal. Sometimes during difficult times, staying focused and being disciplined require you to believe in yourself. Even in times of doubt, you need to believe in your ability. Always tell yourself that you can do it. You'll be surprised by how much of an impact it has on your goals and your confidence.

Conclusion

To be a high performer, you have to be passionate about the goal. Passion is not something that comes down to you. It is something that you generate yourself. I feel that following the elements I discussed will lead to greater passion for your goals. Most things in life are not given; they are acquired. So it is with passion.

Chapter 10

Identifying and Capitalizing on Opportunities

To be successful, you need to be able to capitalize on your opportunities. Opportunities often knock on our doors very softly. Sometimes opportunity comes to us in the midst of crisis. Knowing how to identify opportunity and capitalize on it is an art most high performers are good at. Like most success principles, it is a form of art that is acquired. To master this skill of identifying and capitalizing on opportunity, you must master the skill of preparation. Let's explore how to develop this skill.

Luck

Luck is when preparation meets opportunity.

When someone gets a lot of opportunities, we sometimes call them lucky. In my opinion, there are different forms of luck. The form of luck relating to opportunity is different. The Roman philosopher Seneca said that luck is when preparation meets opportunity. High performers who are lucky do a great deal of work to control their luck. Some of them do it knowingly, and some do it unknowingly. How do they control their luck? They do it by simply preparing for the opportunity, which all of us can do.

Luck can be controlled. This is contrary to the popular belief that luck is something you have. I believe you can influence your outcome and change your luck. You control your luck by being proactive and choosing well. In Chapter 6, "Being Proactive," I discuss being proactive in more depth. On your road to success, you have to be able to influence your luck.

You can influence luck to turn your way.

You can influence luck in the following ways:

Acting: When you see opportunities, you need to act. Of course you need to have plans, but you need to act and execute those plans. If you don't properly execute your plans, they will be ineffective. When you see opportunities on the horizon, you have to act to prepare for those opportunities. You have to have plans to prepare for them and execute your plans right away. You might not have time to prepare for an opportunity once it is already there. You need to learn to anticipate your opportunity and prepare for it now. You can see the corporate version of this play out with new market opportunities: The corporations that are not prepared to serve a new customer base or get to market first with a product lose out on market share as a result. The "lucky" companies get the business instead.

Strategizing: Once you see an opportunity on the horizon, put a strategy in place to seize that opportunity. The strategy is your approach to prepare for this opportunity. It is a gamble and a risk to prepare for an opportunity that is not here, but this is what success means. You have to take calculated risks.

Being proactive: Strategizing and acting are essentially being proactive. Being proactive means doing what is required to capitalize on the opportunity that is on the horizon. You need to go out of your way to prepare for the opportunity. It is difficult and takes effort.

Opportunity

Let's try to define opportunity. One way to look at opportunity is to look at it as a chance to grow and go beyond who you are right now. Opportunities are chances to take you from where you are today to a better place. It is a chance to take you forward. Thus, when opportunity knocks on our door, we need to harness every resource to seize it. It will take us to the next level. If we miss opportunity, we will stagnate where we are.

Every day new opportunities come our way. Most of the time, we don't see many of our opportunities as real opportunities. They pass us by without our even realizing that they were opportunities. Blame human nature for our neglect of them. In order for us to pick up even a fraction of the opportunities, we have to be really alert and attuned.

Have you noticed that children pick up on a lot of things from their surroundings? Children notice things that adults would hardly notice. As we grow up, we learn to filter things out and focus on what is important to us. Children don't have these filters in place yet. As a result, they see everything. The filters that we have are our perceptions. Our perceptions cloud our view of the world and show us only what we want to see. As a result, we see only a fraction of the opportunities that fall within the scope of our perception.

 In order to see opportunities, you need to recognize that your perception is not the only way of seeing the world.

In order for us to recognize opportunities for what they are, we need to look beyond our perception. Perceptions can be changed. We need to accept the fact that there could be other perceptions out there in the world and that ours is only one out of 7 billion. It is only when we start seeing the world from different views that we open ourselves to many opportunities.

The figure below shows how different people's perceptions would see the same opportunity in different ways. Consider a marketing opportunity for cell phones. Each of us would see the opportunity in different ways, thereby seeing the market from different perspectives.

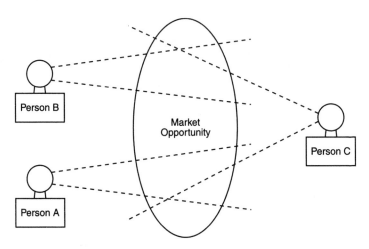

Both person A and B would see only a narrow segment of the market, but each would see different segments of the market. Person A might see the data segment of the market by positioning cell phone technology for portable Internet connections. Person B might see voice opportunity by seeing the potential in voice communications. Person C could see the entire market by taking feedback from both Person A and B and could see the combined possibilities in the market and their synergies. Person C, who is open to many different perspectives, could see a large section of the market and most of the opportunities within that market.

We all need to be more like Person C. Though initially we don't want to see different perspectives, we have to be open to them. We need to listen to different perspectives without being judgmental. We have to try to view others' perspectives and look at the opportunities from others' perspectives.

We as humans have evolved to selectively see what we want to see. Because of this mechanism, most of the opportunities that pass in front of us don't get recognized as opportunities. You have probably noticed that in crisis situations, we tend to capitalize on opportunities more than when there is no crisis. We tend to solve problems better in urgent or critical situations than we do in relaxed times. We ask ourselves, "Why didn't we see this coming?" or "Why couldn't I solve this earlier?" You didn't see it coming simply because you are human.

During crisis situations, we focus our attention selectively to look at opportunities and solutions to solve the current crisis. Our attention is focused on the current crisis. In ordinary times, our attention is not focused on that problem. This is why we do not see opportunities coming.

Wanting a Specific Goal

So how do you prepare for opportunities? You have to have the "need" to move in a certain direction, and you should have made up your mind about it. For example, if you want to lose some weight, you genuinely need to have the desire to lose it. Most everyone would like to lose a few pounds, but very few of us actually want to do what it takes to lose a few pounds. This is why there is a billion-dollar weight-loss industry. There is a big difference between liking something and wanting something.

Liking something comes from your logic and mind, but wanting comes from your emotions. Wanting is a burning desire to achieve your goal. When you want something, you usually get it. You never give up when you want something, but you might easily give it up if you just like something. This desire takes you through the rough times as it is about passion for what you want. Fortunately, like most things in this world, wanting is an acquired skill.

You have to be committed and persistent to achieve your goals.

If you want something, you should be committed to obtaining it and be persistent. It's about telling yourself, "I will achieve this goal no matter what happens" and truly believing it. When there are difficult times, it's about persistence. When things are going well for us, it is very difficult to tell the difference between what you want and what you like. Only when things get difficult does the difference between what you like and what you want become evident. So, develop a passion for what you want.

As humans, we have limited capacity, no matter how brilliant we are. We can like millions of things, but we can be passionate and want only a few things. The more we add to the list of what we want, the more we dilute our passion.

Defining Goals and Preparing for Them

It is very important to define what you want. If you want to lose weight, start by defining how much you plan to lose and thinking of a high-level approach. You need to mentally prepare yourself for what you want, when you want it, and what your strategy will be. When you have done this, you'll have about 80 percent of your preparation complete.

Let's look at how preparation works. No matter how sharp we are, humans have evolved to selectively pay attention to specific issues. This mechanism helps us focus well and has aided in our survival over time. At the same time, it filters out most of the opportunities that come our way. When we don't focus on our goal, opportunities pass by us every day. Only after they've passed do we sometimes realize their potential.

When we want something and we are passionate about something, our selective-attention mechanism automatically gives our attention to any opportunity that comes our way and relates to our goal. We immediately identify the opportunity. This way, we can capitalize on it and use the opportunity to achieve our goal.

Changing my career from engineering to accounting is an example. A few years into my career, I realized that I liked finance and accounting. After having studied engineering and marketing and putting enormous effort and resources into those careers, I felt that getting a finance job was a remote possibility, especially in a middle-management position. My only option was to start fresh. But I still wanted to be an accountant. Because of my desire to be an accountant, I took accounting courses and did my exams part time. When I moved to a new country, I found out that the technology and marketing job markets were saturated. However, there were plenty of finance jobs around. My accounting training gave me the preparation I needed to capitalize on this opportunity, even though I didn't exactly know at the time what kind of job I'd get.

Preparation is all about developing a passion toward the goal. It is our selective attention that keeps us away from most of our opportunities. To prepare for opportunities, you need to want something. You need to passionately want to achieve your goal. When we passionately want something, we start seeing opportunities and also preparing ourselves for any possible opportunities that come our way.

The Remaining 20 Percent

Once we decide to move toward a goal, we need to invest time, effort, and money into that goal. This is the remaining 20 percent of your journey.

Prepare yourself for the opportunities that you want to capitalize on.

Preparing ourselves for possible opportunities is a risk. You always face the risk of not having any opportunities come your way. The relationship between risk and return is directly proportional. The greater the risk you take, the higher the return. There are times when we should not take the risk. However, risk taking in preparation for an opportunity certainly yields a lot of return.

We are all generally risk averse. It's within our nature not to take risk. We don't generally take risks even when it would benefit us. Our society teaches us not to take risks. This is ingrained in our upbringing. However, high performers are people who take selected risks. They take calculated risks. Very few of us do this. This is why only a few of us become leaders, millionaires, and CEOs.

Part of this preparation is to evaluate this risk. Though we need to take risk, I do not recommend taking risk blindly, like putting all your savings in risky stock investments. We need to evaluate the risk vs. the return. Should we need to invest time and energy, we can do that.

Furthermore, we should not put off preparation because there is no foreseeable opportunity. Opportunity might come now, tomorrow, next week, or even ten years from now. When the opportunity comes, if we are prepared, then we can take advantage. Just because the opportunity is not there doesn't mean we should stop preparing. We wouldn't be able to capitalize on the opportunity if we weren't prepared.

Risk Taking

 Success is about taking calculated risks.

In order to capitalize on opportunities, you need to take calculated risks. My father was a risk-averse person. He always told me, "Try to avoid risks." Contrary to this advice, I always took risks, which were, however, calculated. I am not the kind of person who would take blind risks, but I did jump on opportunities based on gut feeling. There were times when the risks that I took were mistakes, but most of the time, I was able to succeed because of the risks that I took. In fact, later in life I realized that it is important to take risks. You cannot live without taking risks. Without taking risks, you cannot succeed in life. The opportunities in life will not wait for you until you do all the analysis and feel safe. You have to jump on to the train when the time is right. For this, you have to be fearless. You have to make a choice and move forward.

We can learn a lot about taking risk by studying risk management from the business world. Risk management is its own profession, but let me give you the basics of risk taking. Risk is essentially a chance that the outcome you expect will be incorrect: either it will result in a loss, or it will pay off to a greater degree than you expected (in which case you have little to worry about). This is called a deviation from your goal. Let's say you want to earn $70,000 in five years. It is possible you might earn only $40,000, and it is also possible that you might earn $90,000. You are currently earning $50,000 in a stable job. There is a business opportunity that will pay you $150,000 if everything goes right but only $40,000 if things may go wrong. You would be taking a risk by pursuing that opportunity because you might earn only $40,000.

Whenever you face a risk, you have several options. Take a look at these options from our example above:

Avoid the risk: You could avoid the risk completely by not taking the opportunity. Of course, by avoiding, you will not receive the potential benefits of the opportunity. Not only are you avoiding the downside, you are also avoiding the upside. So you will earn what you are earning today.

Reduce/mitigate the risk: You could take the risk and do something to avoid the downside. This requires you to think creatively and strategize. Let's say your spouse is staying at home. He or she could start working so that in case your opportunity goes in the wrong direction, there is a second income to support you. However, when you mitigate the risk, you also lose a bit of the upside. For example, if you have kids, now you would have to pay for a babysitter, which means you might earn $150,000 but that your final take-home would be lower because of higher expenses.

Transfer the risk: In this option, you would transfer the risk to someone else. This especially relates to the downside. Let's say there is an insurance company that would pay you if something went wrong with your new business. You buy an insurance policy that would cover you against business losses in your new opportunity. Now you have transferred your risk to someone else, i.e., the insurance company. Of course, there would be a cost involved in this option too. You would have to pay regular premiums to the insurance company, similar to your babysitting costs from the previous option.

Accept/Retain: Here you would accept the downside of earning only $40,000 and move forward with the risk. Of course, on the upside, you could gain $150,000.

The four aspects of risk can be summarized in the following spectrum of choices.

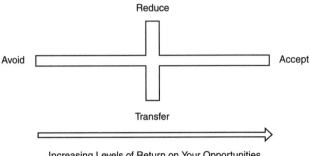

All our choices fit into one of these categories. Any choice that you take would have its costs and its benefits. So you need to weigh the costs and benefits to understand what choice you should make. Our choices define us. What choice would you make based on what you want in life?

Conclusion

We all know that opportunity knocks on our door quietly. We need to be able to see this opportunity coming. This is a skill that you can develop. To develop the ability to see and capitalize on opportunities, we first need to have a goal and develop a passion to run toward that goal. This is 80 percent of the work. The remaining 20 percent is investing time, effort, and money to prepare for possible opportunities. The risk that you take to prepare is worth it. It will make you a high performer.

CHAPTER 11

HAVING A POSITIVE ATTITUDE

L ife does not always go as planned. There are times when we win, and there are times when we lose, whatever the situation. We need to remain positive, not only when things go right but also when things go wrong. Having a positive attitude is not just saying positive words to cover your negative feelings. It means believing that things will work out in the end.

Life is never easy. Sometimes people take life for granted and talk about it as if it should be easy, but there will always be problems and difficulties. It is through difficulties that we grow and mature. During difficult times, it is our nature to feel frustrated and negative. But difficult times always pass away, and good times always come back. If we are to attain any form of success, we need to change our negative thoughts and attitudes to positive ones during these challenging times.

Why Maintain a Positive Attitude?

The reasons for having the correct attitude should be obvious. A positive attitude is a must for success. There is a 1:1 correlation between your attitude and success. It's surprising how few people understand this even though they know the principle. Knowing and understanding are two different things. Our attitude affects our success in many different ways.

Our environment and the people around us respond to our attitude.

Our environment responds to our attitude. How many times have you worked around your boss's mood? You might even plan certain decisions around his or her mood. Our attitude has a direct impact on our surroundings and people around us. Even if we don't speak a word, anyone can sense our attitude. When we do speak to someone, we instinctively know their attitude, and most of the time we adjust our message accordingly. We all know that if we have a positive environment around us, it will give us positive results. For example, when we have happy employees, they do better work. When we have a happy family, we enjoy more comfort at home. On the flip side, when employees feel unhappy, they are stressed, and their creativity is scuttled. When you don't have a creative workforce, you don't have productivity and very little problem solving. Our attitude has a major impact on our surroundings.

Our relationships feed off our attitude. People who have positive attitudes naturally attract people and friends. Your friends will get closer to you because it is human nature to like people who have positive attitudes. It feels satisfying to complain about our problems, feel bad about ourselves, and have people feel sorry and listen to us. But in the long run, that actually pushes people away. While friends would sympathize for a while, nobody likes to hear about someone else's problems on an ongoing basis. Even in your relationship with your spouse, your attitude determines how strong your relationship becomes. Again, it might feel satisfying to always complain about your problems and vent to your spouse, but in the long run you might actually be hurting your relationship with your spouse. It is difficult for anyone to listen to a negative attitude for a prolonged period. You need to put yourself in the other person's position to understand how it gets received.

Our relationships and environment lead to the results that we get, thereby affecting our success. To be successful, you need to get results with your goals. You need to have a positive attitude so that you can have good relationships and a productive environment to catapult you to success.

Success depends on the attitude we have.

To succeed in life, you have to be positive. This chapter explores why it is important to maintain a positive attitude and how to develop a positive attitude.

The Attitude Bridge

What is thinking positively? It is about having hope and looking at things from a different perspective. If you truly look back at all your difficult times, you will notice that good things always followed difficult times. Difficult times don't last forever. Maintaining a positive attitude is about being able to focus on the good times ahead rather than the difficult times you're going through.

> The bridge between past and present is you. You have the choice to make your future different from your past.

We all see things through lenses. We have perceptions of things that get formed as we grow up. These perceptions shape the decisions we make and how we react to opportunities. These perceptions from our past directly affect our future. However, one thing you have to realize: the bridge between the past and the future is you. The choice remains with you. Though past events have created certain perceptions inside you, you can always change these perceptions by making a choice. A positive attitude and having hope are important factors affecting your destiny.

Difficult situations can really throw us off our tracks. It is during difficult times that having a positive attitude really helps. We can have all the great plans and goals in the world, yet life sometimes throws curve balls at us. We need to have a positive attitude during these times because it can really throw us off track.

Let's say you are on track to lose weight. Due to an emergency meeting, you have to fly to a different part of the world, where you could not get the foods you need for your diet. Do you throw away your diet because of this situation? No. You need to have a positive attitude and be positive that you are going to achieve your goal.

Achieving goals is difficult. If you think positively that you are going to achieve your goal, you will. It will take you through the difficult times.

 Every situation has at least two sides. Thinking positively is about seeing the positive side of every situation.

Every situation can have both a good side and a bad side. Thinking positively is all about seeing the positive side of every situation. A positive attitude helps you to be persistent in your goals. You have to have persistence because you are bound to fail in your goals a few times. You need to think of the end result that you stand to gain. You need to think all the great things you are going to achieve. Believe in yourself. People who succeed seldom succeed on their first try. However, they don't generally talk about all the failed attempts. You need to forget about the negative thoughts and start thinking positively.

Sometimes, thinking positively will change your attitude toward taking risk. As humans, we all have different preferences for the level of risks we can handle in our everyday lives. Thinking positively will make you take more calculated risks than thinking negatively. You will have better rewards when you take better risks. You tend to overestimate the risks when you have a negative attitude. I am not saying that we will all start jumping off bridges with bungee cords. But you will start seeing the light at the end of the tunnel when we think of things more positively.

As discussed in a previous chapter, your attitude affects your ability to take risk. In order to succeed and move toward your goals, you need to take calculated risks. When you have a positive attitude, it helps to evaluate your risks more effectively. Risk taking rests on your perception of what the outcome is going to be. If you perceive your outcome to be negative, then you will be reluctant to take the risk. Alternatively, if you perceive the outcome to be positive, then you will take the risk. It is viewing whether the glass is half empty or half full. The same situation can be viewed in two different ways.

For example, imagine that you are investing in the stock market. If you view the signs in the market as gloomy, then you will not take the risk of investing your money. If you view the market to be bullish, then you will invest your money.

Having a positive attitude is a habit. Over time, we get used to thinking about things positively. This habit of how we perceive things is mainly a result of what has happened in our lives before, our experiences, and our behavior.

Our upbringing and history play a major role in how we perceive things in life. If you had a wonderful childhood, a good set of friends, and successful achievements in your life, it is likely that you see the positive side of things all the time. This is because you have seen mostly positive things in life. This attitude will result in more positive things coming your way, and you will have established that things in life are generally positive even when things go wrong. You will know that when there is a downturn, there is always an uptick that you can enjoy.

On the contrary, if you had a difficult childhood, difficult marriage, and difficult history, it is likely that you see things negatively. The map of your world will be different, and that's okay. A bit of a negative attitude can sometimes be useful in life. To take better advantage of the power of positive thinking, however, you can always develop a new map, if you are willing. Positive thinking is a habit. New habits can be learned and unlearned.

To always see the positive side of things, you need to change. You need to develop a deep desire to change. The fact that you're reading this book is a testament to that desire. This is very important. Everything else depends on it. Start looking at each situation in life, and think about the positive things that have happened in your life. Let's say you missed an examination because you were late. Think about how you could study more next time and be prepared better. You could be surer of yourself next time.

Try to think of the good things that can happen with any situation. In the first few days of change, it might seem like trying to swim against the current. It might seem very artificial to you. However, after a few days, it should come more naturally. You will shift your focus to being more positive when things work out for you.

Everybody has problems in life, but what makes people different is their attitude toward their problems. You have the power to choose. There are people who believe that problems and issues are the end and that they are destined to have them. They believe that there is no solution to these problems. Then there are others who always carry hope and rise out of these problems.

When you have a positive attitude, you see beyond the problem. You look at ways of solving it. Problems are opportunities. Positive people don't see a problem as an end. Instead, they see solutions. They see problems more as hurdles that need to be climbed over to get to their destination. Having a positive attitude gives you this energy, energy to look beyond problems and issues and focus on the goal.

Looking at situations negatively is very easy. It does not take much emotional energy to think negatively. It is self-fulfilling and provides an excuse not to reach beyond. This is why we gravitate toward negativity. The more we gravitate toward negativity, the more it becomes a habit, like smoking. Smoking becomes a habit and an addiction because people get attracted to it and it is easy. By human nature, we like the easy way out.

By contrast, having a positive attitude requires energy and effort. You need to make an effort to stay motivated. You need to make an effort to think through possible solutions. You need to make an effort to just stay afloat during difficult times.

 Your attitudes are contagious.

Your attitudes are contagious in your relationships. You don't have to say a word for your attitude to be adopted by another person. If you have a positive attitude, your family and your coworkers will sense it.

You will have a healthier marriage because a) you will infect your spouse with your positive attitude and b) you will look at your lives and problems in terms of wonderful things and solutions. It's much easier to build relationships with people when you are positive. We like people who are upbeat and positive. So having a positive attitude will win a lot of hearts.

Your children will grow up being very successful and positive if you have a positive attitude. They are like sponges absorbing the nonverbal signals that you give out. The most important one is your attitude toward life. Children are the ones who will absorb most of your attitudes. They try to mirror you all the time.

In turn, you will have more reason to be positive as it has a spiraling effect. Being positive makes you more positive. It is a vicious cycle!

The Cycle of Attitude

Our attitude is cyclical. Once we have a positive attitude, the cycle gets activated, and it results in your having a better attitude than you started off with. Based on your experience, you can draw this cycle as follows:

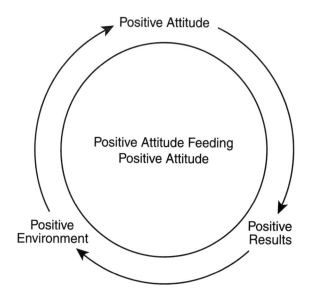

Positive Attitude

Positive Attitude Feeding
Positive Attitude

Positive
Environment

Positive
Results

Our thoughts and perceptions form our attitude. By controlling our thoughts, we can control our attitude.

The cycle has three main components:

1. **Our attitude:** On a daily basis, our thoughts and perceptions form our attitude. Our attitude is not something that comes to us. We create it with the thoughts that we have and the perceptions that we have. Based on our thoughts and perceptions, we have feelings. These feelings form our attitude. Thoughts and perceptions are completely within our control, and therefore our attitude is completely within our control.

   For example, if we perceive that the world is going to end, we are going to feel terrible and have a bad attitude. Alternatively, if we look around ourselves and see the big picture of life continuing, we will feel different and have a different attitude.

   We see what we want to see. As humans, we have selective sight and selective hearing. We filter things out. So if we want to have a positive attitude, we will start seeing positive things around us and in turn, we will feel different and our attitude will be different. Our attitude is based on what we want in life. If we want problems, we will have problems. If we want a great life, we will have a great life. The choice is ours.

2. **Results:** Based on our attitude, we influence the results that we get. The relationships that we have will be more positive, thereby adding value to relationships with peers and friends. Also, when you have a positive attitude, you find the motivation and energy to accomplish much more. Motivation is a key ingredient to getting things done. As humans, we can't do anything that we are not motivated to do. When we have a positive attitude, you will be motivated to get more things done.

For example, if you have the attitude that your job is terrible, you might perceive that your supervisor is out to get you, thereby demeaning your motivation to get things done. If your results are not good, your supervisor could start managing you differently from other employees, making it even more difficult for you to get motivated and get things done.

Your attitude has a direct impact on your results. Your motivation rests on your attitude and affects achievement and energy level.

3. **Environment:** When your results are bad, your relationships tend to suffer and make your environment a less pleasant place. For example, when you can't deliver results and have unsatisfactory pay, you will have financial difficulties. This might cause problems in your family life because you can't do what you like to do (such as going on vacation), thereby making your environment at home a bad place.

Your environment in turn feeds your attitude, making you feel worse.

When you have a great attitude, you will have great results, and people will be attracted to you. You will have friends and family around you making you feel great. This in turn will make your attitude even better.

This is the cycle of attitude. You can always break away from this cycle. To break away, you need only to change. Change the core determinants of your attitude: your perceptions and thoughts.

Being negative has the same impact, except in the opposite direction. People don't like negative people. So you will create unnecessary difficulty in your relationships. You don't have to say a word to pass on your negative attitude. It will get passed on automatically. People around you will sense your negativity. Instead of gravitating toward you, they will more likely turn away. Think of a day when your boss was in a bad mood and how it affected you and your coworkers. Likewise, your children will absorb your negative attitude, and they in turn will be more likely to look at things negatively. The cycle affects the people around you, so you need to break out of it.

Conclusion

Ultimately, a negative attitude affects your overall quality of life, performance, opportunities, and success. This is why you need to break out of the negative cycle. Initially, it will seem artificial and difficult. Keep at it. It will certainly make your life a lot better. Negativity does not get you anywhere. If you want to be successful, a positive attitude is crucial.

CHAPTER 12

WINNING IN THE
LONG RUN

In life, we all need to win. Victory is what we are all after. There are all types of victories. The ultimate victory is what matters to us most. The reason you're reading this book is because you want to achieve goals in life and win. All of us want to be victorious in our lives. Yet, in the midst of achieving these goals, we sometimes lose track of the true meaning of winning.

What really is winning? Winning in the long run means achieving your ultimate goal—happiness. We all set goals, and we strategize to achieve these goals. Our journey in life is a complex one. Each of us has a different set of problems and opportunities no matter how blessed or cursed we think we are. Yet one thing every one of us has in common is that we all strive to be happy.

Achieving happiness is our ultimate goal. Everything we do, we do to achieve happiness. Winning in the long run means achieving this ultimate goal. Our journey in life is to achieve this ultimate goal. There's no one in this world for whom happiness is not the ultimate goal. From the orphan in Africa to the CEO on Wall Street, we all seek the same thing in some form or another in our lives.

The goals that you set in life play an important role in this journey. To achieve happiness, you need to set your goals carefully and achieve them. More important, you need to define what ultimate happiness means to you. Winning in the long run is all about achieving this ultimate goal through a series of smaller goals. Your definition of happiness might sound like a pie-in-the-sky concept, yet you have to know what you're trying to achieve. Everything else in life flows from this definition.

Every time we win, we have to win against some competition. And when we win, we cannot take all the winnings with us. We need to ensure that we don't undermine relationships and leave a bad after-taste. Everybody needs to win something. Successful leaders ensure this happens when they win.

Winning also means doing things in a balanced way. Life is one big balancing act. Life is full of things that you need to balance, and there is never a correct formula to apply in each situation. You have to use your judgment and common sense to determine this balance. Is it ever easy? No, if life were easy, we'd all have wonderful lives! A wonderful life demands work.

Winning is complex. It means doing the right things in life so that it becomes meaningful. In this chapter, we'll explore the concept of winning.

Material Success

In this modern world, we tend to associate material success with happiness. In some cases, this is true. Materialistic success, such as having a wonderful house or a large bank account, can lead to security and satisfaction, but it can't make you happy. The financial crisis of 2008 is a testament to this false association.

 Material success rarely is a means to an end.

We make a lot of choices based on this false assumption, especially when it comes to careers. Many jobs undoubtedly force people to make compromises between family and job, but to make this compromise only for material gain is misguided. Always keep your final goal and the purpose behind it in mind.

Material goals should never be a means to an end. We set material goals in hopes that there will be happiness at the end of the tunnel. When we compromise happiness to achieve this goal, our lives stop making sense. This is why we sometimes feel that we are in a constant cycle of traveling but not getting anywhere. We are being very efficient, but not effective. We might be feeling rich but not happy.

We might have all the latest gadgets but not the happiness we are seeking. You might know of people who don't have much compared to you but are very content. You see the happiness in their eyes, and you wonder how they do it.

They do it by focusing on the ultimate goal. In the materialistic world that we live in, we are under constant pressure to achieve materialistic success. Most of the time, the materialistic success does not equate to the ultimate goal of happiness.

In search of success, we get confused with what is effective and what is efficient. The wealth that we accumulate is efficient; if we are not doing it to achieve our ultimate goal of happiness, however, then it is not effective. Working hard to do something or achieve something might be efficient and would get you to your immediate goal, but if the immediate goal does not contribute to your ultimate success, then you are not being very effective.

Losing a Battle to Win a War

We sometimes need to lose the battle to win the war. Achieving your goals is the same thing. You sometimes have to give up certain short-term wins for the sake of long-term wins. It is walking away from an argument rather than getting in the last word. This is much easier said than done. Our human tendency is to win all the time. We have to resist the temptation and walk away; walk away and restrategize. There is always more than one way of doing things. The world is an abundant place. It is just a matter of time until you realize an alternate way.

I personally have this tendency to always get in the last word. Somehow, I can never seem to let go. I want to win the argument. In situations where I have won, I realize that I have in fact lost. This is important especially in marriages. If your goal is to have a wonderful family life, you have to learn to lose a lot of short-term battles to win the war in the long run. You can win an argument by getting out what's in your mind, but you will realize that it takes much longer to heal. Sometimes, it might never heal at all. We are all human. In getting to our ultimate goal, we make mistakes and take wrong turns.

Losing a battle or two in the short run is about correcting these mistakes and taking a different approach. It is about analyzing our choices against a framework of our ultimate goal of happiness. We all have to do it.

Persistence vs. Reevaluation

You need to be persistent about your goals. Your plans will fail because there are many factors in each plan and it is impossible to factor everything at the inception. Persistence is the only way you will achieve your goal and win. Take Thomas Edison; if he hadn't been persistent, someone else would have invented the light bulb. We need to push to achieve our goals. When we believe in our goals, we keep at it rather than giving up.

There are times when you have to give up a short-term win and restrategize because it is simply not working. We are reluctant to give up, but when something isn't working, we have to give up.

There is a subtle difference between persistence and the need to reevaluate. When you are persistent, you know that you are doing the right thing, but when you need to reevaluate, you instinctively sense that things are not working. There are times when being persistent will actually hurt your end result. You need to find alternative ways when this happens. We all need to use our best judgment in every case. There is no formula. We simply have to make the effort to make the correct choice.

Say you travel to work with your spouse and get to work late every day because of the way your spouse drives. Your goal is to get to work on time so that you can get your things done. You have tried to change his or her way of driving, and it isn't working. You can be persistent and put your marriage in trouble. Or you can find a different way to work, such as public transit. Though this might be insignificant in the overall scheme of things, it could be the tipping point between a good marriage and a bad marriage.

You need to know how important your win will be relative to your ultimate goal. If you will be happy with a good marriage, then you need to give up trying to change his or her driving habits. Again, strategy and creativity are important tools for finding alternatives.

Competition

Everybody needs to win. If you are the only one who gains something from a situation, then you have not won.

On the road to success, we are all going to meet competition because there are always fewer opportunities for success than there are willing people. Most of us don't like to face competitive situations because we don't want to confront a difficult situation. But if you are to succeed, this is one trait you need to develop. You need to win against your competition. At the same time, dealing with competition is a delicate balance. Many competitive situations will result in a winner and a loser. The thing to keep in mind when you emerge the winner is that your competition shouldn't feel like they lost. You can't bulldoze your peers at work for being your competition. At some point in your career, your paths might cross again. You need to handle competition tactfully.

In competitive situations, each person needs to gain something from the situation. You lose relationships when you win to the exclusion of everyone else. Everybody needs to feel they've won something. Succeeding gracefully is the art of winning.

For example, let's say you get promoted to department manager. Most of your colleagues were also aiming for the same job. Once you get the job, you could give them a raise and expand their responsibilities so that they don't feel they have lost the race. You need to gain hearts of minds. Good leaders and successful high performers do this very well. Only the short-sighted winners take it all.

The Importance of Relationships

Relationships are far more important than material success.

We live in an interconnected world. This is why all new technologies that enable enhanced communication boom instantly. To achieve your ultimate goal, you need relationships. Severing relationships will not give you happiness. You might achieve your immediate goal, but you will have lost in the long run.

I remember trying to get my first promotion. I tried to make my mark in the organization by making one of my colleagues give up his contingency on his project. I did make my mark by saving a few hundred thousand dollars and getting my promotion, but I was never able to have a truthful relationship with this gentleman because I broke his trust. Once broken, trust in a relationship seldom returns to the level you started off with. It was then that I realized that winning in the long run is more important than winning in the short run. When in doubt, take the relationship over the goal. You can always set new goals and restrategize on how to achieve them, but it is very difficult to restore relationships.

This concept becomes very important with marriage. People initially get married for the physical, sexual, and mental attraction. Though we are led to believe by society that this is love, unfortunately, this attraction lasts only a certain period of time no matter how attractive we are. Beyond that, true love really is a choice that we make. A large part of this choice is a sacrifice for the good of the relationship. To win in your marriage in the long run and be happy, you first need to lose by giving yourself up.

Relationships are your primary vehicle for success. The saying "no person is an island" is very true. We get things done with the help of others, and we learn about opportunities through others. We cannot live in a world of our own.

Too many people view relationships as transactional. Transactional means that you get something out of the relationship. We all are in relationships because of mutual benefit, but we should not make relationships transactional. Rich relationships have both sacrifice and benefit components. You give something and get something as well. Rich relationships offer a lot more synergy and productivity.

The reason that so many people view relationships as transactional is they're always thinking about their benefit. In other words, we are selfish. It is in our nature to be selfish because it ensures our survival. Though we all feel selfish at times, we must work to overcome this feeling. Again, it is a choice we make. We can either let our feelings overcome us or we can make the effort to overcome our feelings. It is the latter that leads us to success. Because when we do overcome our selfish feelings, we have better relationships that are based on not only taking but also giving. These rich relationships will take you closer to your success.

Abundance

 There is an abundance of opportunities. You only need to look for them.

Always know that there is an abundance of opportunities in the world for everyone. It doesn't have to be that one single job opportunity that you should go for or that one house you should buy. Your perception needs to open when you are trying to win. There are many ways to win what you want and achieve your goal. If the path you are taking is going to damage relationships and burn bridges, consider taking an alternative path to achieve your goals. Chapter 10, "Identifying and Capitalizing on Opportunities," discusses this process in detail. It is important that you be creative with strategy to achieve your goals. Your strategy needs to put a priority on maintaining your relationships and winning in the long run.

Letting everyone around you lose while you win is not really winning; it is grabbing things selfishly. If you are a high performer, avoid this at all costs. Recognize others for their contribution in your win, and let the people who didn't win have something as well.

Conclusion

Success is only success if happiness is attached to it. If happiness is not attached to any achievement, it cannot be called successful. It is just an accomplishment. If happiness is missing from your achievements, there is something very wrong with your achievements. The question comes up, "Why did you spend all the time and effort to achieve something if it does not make you happy?" Sometimes seeking both happiness and success can limit what you accomplish, but you have achieved happiness, which is the ultimate goal. You live to be happy. Without happiness, your achievements don't mean a thing.

If you boil down all your goals and aspirations, the point is to make you happy. So the goals that you set are in fact intermediate steps to your ultimate goal—happiness. Achieving your goals without happiness is wasting your effort for no reason. You might achieve a lot of things in life, but for what?

CHAPTER 13

THE IMPORTANCE
OF NETWORKING

You succeed through your network of relationships. I cannot stress enough the importance of networking. It is an immensely important piece that affects your success. There have been hundreds of books on networking. Though we'll discuss networking in this chapter, it would be beneficial to learn more on this subject if you are just getting exposed to it.

Networking is about keeping in touch with people.

Networking is not a science. Though a lot of people make it sound complicated, it is immensely easy. Networking is essentially knowing people and being in touch with people. I know some of us don't like networking because of the difficulty in talking to strangers. But, if you are to be successful, this is something you need to learn and be comfortable doing. Regardless of our personality types, we all feel the same way about meeting new people.

There are several ways to network. There are networking events, office parties, one-on-one meetings, and Internet sites. It is all about getting to know other people and adding value to their lives. Any way you could get to know someone is a way of networking.

Networking gives you confidence about yourself. The more people you meet, the wider your safety net will be to go to for help when you need it. When you talk with people, you will start realizing your own accomplishments and the value that you add. You can actually discover yourself through your networking. Once you start receiving feedback from people, you'll learn about your strengths and opportunities.

Networking can also fulfill your purpose. We all need to add value to our environment. Networking gives us the opportunity to do exactly this. When we meet people who need help, we can put our strengths to work by helping them. We will see opportunities in which we can shine. You could add tremendous value to others through networking, and it will help fulfill your purpose. It is very rewarding. When we do help people, we feel valued and appreciated. This feeling is important as it ties back to our self-worth and self-confidence.

Let's discuss the important aspects of networking so that you understand how it plays into your success.

Networking and Relationships

You cannot succeed without people. Networking enables you to be in touch with people.

Success depends on our relationships. To succeed, we need to have opportunities and resources. It is through relationships that we gain both of these. Relationships enable us to both give and also receive.

As humans, we need to add value to our environment. The technology and creature comforts that we have today came from the people here before us who added value to the world through various contributions. For us to add value, we need to work with others.

Also, we gain through our relationships. We gain friendship, emotional support, and encouragement. Though these can never be quantified, they are immensely important for our growth, maturity, and success. Our relationships keep us alive.

When we give value to the people that we know, we in turn receive favors and help. It is through this help that we can succeed. We can never succeed all by ourselves. We need others to succeed.

Networking enables us to do exactly that. Networking enables us to maintain these relationships.

Reputation and Networking

 You build your reputation through your network of people. People would rather work with someone they know than someone they don't.

Your reputation is what people think of you and what they think you can do. If you look at famous people (as opposed to infamous people), they largely have great reputations. We hear about them through our friends, family, and the media. When you have a reputation, you get in touch with so many opportunities. In fact, the reason a lot of famous people can demand large paychecks is because they get so many opportunities because of their reputations that they can actually choose which opportunities to take. Similarly, you need to build your reputation based on what you can do. Your network of contacts is how you build your reputation.

When you have a network of contacts, people get to know what you can do and what value you can add to their lives. This is very important because word of mouth is the most trusted form of marketing for anything. If you can use the power of word of mouth to promote yourself, many opportunities will come your way.

For example, as a hiring manager, I would rather hire someone I know than a fresh, unknown applicant. The reason is I would trust a known person's word more than an unknown person's. With your network of contacts, you can have someone recommend you for a potential job rather than applying for it cold. You have far higher chances of getting a job based on a personal recommendation than you do applying cold.

All of us have accomplishments that prove we have added value. You can use your network to spread the word about your accomplishments. Similar to famous people where everyone knows about their accomplishments, others will get to know your accomplishments, and you can build a reputation more effectively. People will get to know who you are.

People get their first impressions based on various factors. As humans, we form judgments about people based on how we look, the way we talk, and a variety of other ways, yet our networks can help offset any negative impressions people form about us. When those people get to know who you are and the value that you can add in their lives, their impressions change. I have had this happen to me so many times; I would have an impression of someone I had seen that changed after hearing someone shared their impression of the same person with me. We always trust the known over the unknown.

Goal Assistance

We can't succeed on our own. We need help to achieve our goals and succeed. Our network of contacts helps us do this by giving us resources and opportunities. There are several ways in which this happens:

- **Resources and Leverage:** We can obtain help from people who have the skills and abilities to do certain things better than we do. For example, if you want to write a book but aren't good at illustrations, you can use someone in your network to do your illustrations while you craft the content.

- **Synergy:** Your collective ideas could be of far higher quality because there is more than one person thinking at the same time. You could brainstorm and come up with great strategies for your goals by getting help from your network.

- **Influence:** Certain contacts in your network can influence your plan and make it move faster. Let's say you need to get something approved. Often, if you know the administrative assistant of the approver, you can get it approved faster.

- **Delegation:** All our goals are complex projects. In order to achieve them, we need to be able to delegate the work to different people. By having a strong network, you'd be able to delegate work components to people who can do them best.

Opportunities

 Networking is a matching process whereby your strengths are matched with new opportunities, increasing your chances for success.

Of all the reasons you should be networking, the most important is the wealth of opportunities it provides you. In order for you to add value, you have to have opportunities. Your network provides you with countless opportunities because the people you know will know your strengths. You will have opportunities that match your strengths, and you will be able to capitalize on these opportunities well.

Your network of contacts can match you well to unknown opportunities. For example, if there is a job that matches your skill, your network of contacts will likely help you find that opportunity. This matching process is very important because it is through this process that you have opportunities. Without a matching process, you would have to find opportunities on your own, and they could be anywhere. It is similar to door-to-door sales, which can sometimes be very ineffective if you don't have the right product.

How Do You Network?

There are many ways to network. I have read a number of books on networking, and each introduces me to new ways, which are all great ideas. Networking is essentially building and maintaining your contacts. In the process, you add value to their lives. Networking should be done on a continual basis, not just in a time of need. When you network in a time of need, you might actually be doing more harm than good because you are interested only in your advantage. There are a few ways you can achieve this. The following are the three most popular ways to network:

Online: The Internet has become an essential part of our lives. It connects people and makes communication across the world almost seamless. Relationships and communication have gone to a completely new level. It also opens new possibilities for networking: not only through e-mail but also Web sites specifically designed for networking like LinkedIn and Facebook. LinkedIn leans toward professional networking while Facebook is a social-networking site. E-mail, online chatting, and videoconferencing are also tools that enable better networking. Given these fabulous tools available today, you need to learn to master them to network better. Now you can use these tools even on your mobile phone. They are easy to use and convenient.

There will always be new tools coming out, and you need to get in the habit of surveying emerging technologies to see how they can help you. The only certainty in life is change. We all need to get used to learning new things and changing. I sometimes hesitate to use these tools, and then I realize that they are the future of communication. We all need to put effort into learning and changing. It is a choice that we make.

Networking events: Networking events are also great opportunities to network and meet people. The great thing about networking events is that people who attend them come with a networking mindset. Everybody's open to meeting new people and building their network. Moreover, most of these networking events are topic specific, which means people most likely share the same industry or profession as you. This gives you an advantage because everybody talks the same language.

These events let you meet a lot of the people in your area of work so that you can use these contacts to expand your career. Even if you are not in a marketing/sales type of profession or not actively seeking a new job, you should still attend events because you can build a strong network, which you can use when you need.

The only downside is that you have to overcome your shyness of meeting people. In networking events, you see a lot of new faces, and you need to take the initiative to talk to them and meet them.

Your existing contacts: Your existing contacts and friends are the most powerful network you have. Make it a point to develop these contacts and expand this network. These people already know you and can recommend you to other new people. A lot of us think that networking is all about meeting new people and contacts. In fact, it also about maintaining your existing contacts. You need to have a plan and a strategy to maintain your existing network, no matter how small it is. This is a great way to start actively networking. Moreover, you are comfortable with these people because you are familiar with them. When you are just starting to actively network, this can be an advantage.

Maintaining Your Network

Your network of contacts is not something you build when you have a need, such as seeking employment. It should be an ongoing process. Keep in touch with your network of contacts on a regular basis. You don't have to view your network of contacts as separate from your family and friends. They are your friends, and you should be in touch with them.

Maintaining your network is not something to be perceived as a professional obligation. Networking is essentially being a good friend to others. It is being friendly and being a good neighbor. As a good friend, you keep in touch with your friends and are there for them when they need you. That's what they'll remember about you, and that's what networking is all about.

Having a strategy in place to maintain your contacts is very useful. You could have a specific timeframe in mind for networking. I like to make at least one contact every week with someone that I know just to find out how they are doing. This way, you know if they need any help. Anytime you need help, you can always go to these people.

Keeping Promises

 Networking is all about keeping promises, both to yourself and the people on your network.

Keeping promises is very important when it comes to networking. It is important to keep promises to yourself, but it becomes even more important in maintaining your network of contacts. People judge you based on how well you deliver on your promises.

Once you make a promise, you have to deliver on it. There is an instant expectation that is formed when you promise something. You don't have to use the words "I promise ..." to make a promise. When you say, "I'll get it done," you're making a promise. You have to make sure you deliver on that promise once someone has that expectation of you.

Keeping promises to others starts with keeping promises to yourself. If you don't know how to keep promises to yourself, it would be very difficult to keep promises to others. When you make promises to yourself and you break those promises, your self-worth will be severely affected. This in turn will affect how you keep promises to yourself.

Keeping promises has two sides:

1. **Decision:** You make a decision to do something. When you make a decision to do something, you make a promise to yourself. So decide carefully on what you want to do. Because once you say to yourself, "I want to do this ... ," you have made a promise. No matter how you try to forget this, it will be in the back of your mind.

2. **Delivery:** You have to deliver on your promise. You have to get it done for yourself. Let's say you decide to lose weight. You need to make the effort and lose weight. If not, your self-worth will be greatly affected.

Essentially, if you can't deliver, don't decide that you want to do it.

The same principles apply to the people in your network. They expect you to deliver on your promise. So when you say you will get something done, make sure you get it done for them.

Also, it is important to understand what people expect from you. You need to clarify with them what is expected, not only from what was originally said but also not said. A lot of us don't really say outright what we want for many reasons. So it is important to read between the lines and understand what is expected.

While you need to manage expectations, be careful. I've had many bad experiences with people trying to manage my expectations so much that they actually disappointed me instead. Be service-oriented when you are managing expectations. Some of us try to manage expectations by saying, "No, I can't do it" at first and then delivering later on, thereby theoretically exceeding expectations. My question would be, "If you could have done it, why did you say 'no' to start with?" This happens in most customer service departments and call centers. So, you need to be careful in trying to manage expectations. It is a delicate balance like anything else. You should say what you can do rather than trying to exceed expectations at any cost.

When delivering your promises, be responsive. You need to keep people on your network informed of the progress you are making and acknowledge that you understand their expectations. If you don't respond, a lot of people will start thinking that you have forgotten about the promise, even if it takes a long time for you to deliver on your promise.

Overcoming Shyness

A lot of us avoid networking because we're shy. Even if we have outgoing personalities, we are shy in some way. Different people are shy to different degrees. If you actually interview some of the most famous people, even they are shy. Shyness is essentially being self-conscious.

Everybody feels shy sometimes, just as you do.

To overcome your shyness, you need to understand that everybody feels this way. Though a lot of people will come and talk to you, they are shy as well. Make a choice to move forward despite being shy and self-conscious.

When you make the first move to be friendly, you actually spark the conversation. It is the first move that is most difficult. When someone comes and talks to you nicely, you immediately start to respond. It builds from that point onward. The other person probably is also hesitating because he or she is shy as well. Overcome these negative thoughts with positive thoughts. Positive self-talk certainly helps. Tell yourself that you're comfortable talking to a group of people. This actually helps you overcome your shyness.

Whenever I go to a corporate event, I feel shy as well. I think about myself and how others might view me. Recently, I realized that everybody else is feeling the same way. So I made the choice to go out and talk to other people.

Conclusion

Networking is crucial to success. It is through your network that you gain opportunities and resources to achieve your dreams and your goals. There are many ways you can network. In essence, networking is all about keeping in touch with the people you know and getting to know new people. When you are networking, you need to be good at keeping your promises, both to yourself and others. Your credibility is based on promises. Furthermore, you need to overcome your shyness and any negative self-talk. We succeed through people, and without networking, we'd be forced to go it alone.

CHAPTER 14

BEING
SERVICE-ORIENTED

A desire to serve is another one of those critical factors that enables you to be successful. Probably you have been to a store that treated you well and also to a store where the personnel were rude. Which store would you like to visit again? All of us most likely would go back to the store where the service was good!

No matter where we go, it is in our nature to expect good service.

Expecting good service is human nature. We never like people who are rude. Very few people confront and point out that someone is rude. Instead they just don't return if they have a choice. We like people better who are nice to us. The same principle applies in life: in order to succeed, we have to win through others. Being service-oriented means winning through others. You don't have to be in a job that requires you to face customers; you can always help people around you.

I'm sure people who are rude have their reasons, but their chances of becoming successful are slim. This is because they are thinking only about themselves. These folks might get their short-term satisfaction giving others a hard time and feeling superior, but they rarely go far. This is contrary to the notion that successful people are arrogant. Successful people are the ones who are least arrogant, because by being arrogant, you cannot win over people.

You succeed through making others happy.

You gain so much when the people around you are happy. To keep everyone happy, you need to be service-oriented. This does not mean that you have to give up yourself. You need to maintain your self-worth. It just means that you go beyond what is expected of you but without giving the house away. Make some compromises. It is up to us to decide on personal boundaries. Yet you need to know that you cannot keep to yourself and keep people happy.

Also, you become successful by being approachable. Do you like someone whom you cannot approach? Being approachable is a fundamental trait in high performers. By being service-oriented, you become an approachable person. People know that you will help them. That is what is important at the end of the day. You have to care for people. People don't care about how much you know until they know how much you care about them.

Service orientation is essentially being willing to help.

Too few people realize the importance of service orientation in their jobs, at home, and in their communities. People expect service but too rarely want to give it back. Even in a lot of customer service departments, service agents only care about their convenience and their policies. No wonder their competitors steal market share from them. Service orientation is absolutely critical if you want to be successful. Service orientation is just being willing to help, plain human nature.

Listening

One important aspect of being service-oriented is listening to people. All of us know that listening is important, but few of us actually do it. Most of us fake listening. We know the techniques to show how to listen. But to listen is to understand. To be service-oriented, we have to be able to understand the other person. It is only when we understand that we can truly serve him or her.

When we are not listening, it becomes evident. It becomes evident from our body language that we are merely going through the motions. This is worse than avoiding a person because you are actually wasting the other person's time.

When someone talks, we all hear the words. We see the body language, and we can all get the message. But listening is more than hearing and just getting the message. It is empathizing with the other person. When we empathize, we understand not only the situation but also feelings and motives. We see these from another person's perspective. It is difficult for us to see someone else's perspective until we let go of our perspective and truly understand all the dimensions of the situation from another's view.

 We become service-oriented by learning to listen. Listening requires us to put forth effort.

Listening requires us to put forth effort. This is why most people don't listen. It is tiring and draining to pay undivided attention to someone so that we see all the dimensions of their view. But when we do listen, the outcome is rewarding. People start respecting you for listening and become close to you. Sometimes, listening to someone by itself is enough to serve them. In a world filled with messages, very few of us take time to listen. But when we do, people have a lot to share with us.

Giving Feedback

You will rarely get feedback from people when you are not service-oriented. Your network of people will simply turn away and give the opportunities to someone else. You need to understand the reasons why this happens. Finding out why people don't provide feedback is a compelling argument for being more service-oriented. There are situations when people do provide feedback, but these are exceptions.

Psychologically, it is difficult for people to complain and listen to feedback. Most people are reluctant to do it. If you are not empathetic, they will simply go somewhere else. You need to make an effort to provide feedback. When we are young and growing up, we all have experiences when the feedback that we provided went awry. As a result, most of us actually fear giving feedback and facing a confrontation.

It's worse when you're dealing with a coworker. If the relationship goes bad because of unfavorable feedback, you could find yourself in continual confrontations. As a result, you're even less likely to receive feedback from someone you know than from someone you don't.

On the flip side, most of us don't want to hear feedback. To properly receive feedback, we need to consciously let our defenses down. For this, you need to have a deep understanding of yourself and be secure. Most of us don't have the level of security to let our defenses down and receive honest feedback. As a result, we become defensive. Our natural instincts take over, and we end up attacking the person who is giving feedback. This is why most of us have bad experiences with giving feedback.

There are a few exceptions to these situations. Psychologically secure people are more likely to accept feedback well. Another exception for those giving feedback is preparing ahead of time to guard against a defensive reaction. Again, you have to have a strong, secure makeup to do this.

For all these reasons, most people prefer to leave the room than face a difficult, uncomfortable conversation. If you're not being service-oriented, you might not even realize it. Only when the situation gets worse would you find out about it. This is why it's important to be proactively service-oriented. By being service-oriented, you allow your opportunities to come through to you.

Everyone Is a Customer

 Treat everyone like a customer.

The essence of being service-oriented is helping others. It is an age-old philosophy. Every religion preaches this concept in some form or another. However, we rarely practice it. People need people. We cannot live in isolation. When you help others, you become liked by others. When more and more people like you, you become popular. This popularity leads to success.

Certain people try to help only the people above them. They help only people who have some influence. This is also shortsighted. You never know who's climbing up the ladder. Try to help everyone around you. There have been lots of people who never thought that I would be successful in my career.

You need to treat everyone like a customer and the way you'd like to be treated. Not just any customer, but a valuable customer. Be there in their time of need. In the rare case where someone rejects or takes unfair advantage of your help, back out gracefully. However, don't shy away from helping because of a few bad experiences. Most of the people around you genuinely need your help. If you can be there for them, you will definitely win that star in their heart. In certain cultures, people believe that if you help someone genuinely, that deed will follow you and you will receive a deed in return. This is the essence of service orientation.

When helping others and being service-oriented, you need to understand the other person. You don't necessarily need to sympathize, but you need to empathize. There is a big difference between knowing what the other person is going through and understanding it. You can't fake understanding. You can try techniques to make it look like you understand, but the other person would know that you don't. The difference between knowing and understanding is that understanding requires that you appreciate the other person's situation. Simply understanding is sometimes enough to be service-oriented.

Make the other person feel important. As a person, you always want to feel important. So why not make other people feel important? When you make others feel important, you will definitely be important in their lives. No matter how successful you are, everyone wants to feel important. If you can make them feel important, you will always be remembered.

Managing Expectations

Managing expectations is vital to becoming service-oriented.

One of the main aspects of service orientation is managing expectations. The perception of service is relative to expectations. You can deliver good service if you meet or exceed expectations. Managing expectations consists of:

- The commitment that you make
- Your understanding of what is expected
- Feedback
- Delivery

In order to manage expectations, you need to manage all these factors.

Commitment: The commitment you make should be realistic. It should be something that the other person can visualize you achieving. No matter how achievable it is from your perspective, if the other person cannot see it happening, they will not believe you. (Some people have the ability to sell something as realistic, even when it is not.) If the other person cannot visualize it, then you need to help the person visualize it through images. For example, insurance is based on commitment. You cannot see it or feel it, which is why most insurance companies use families and people in their advertising.

It is also important to provide a time line for completion. We tend to say, "I will get it done in the next five days." But interim timetables give people more to go on. You might have said that you will get something done in five days, but if you call within three days and say, "I'm 75 percent done," then the person will have clearer expectations.

When you're making commitments, discuss upfront the effort required for you to deliver. If you promise to make a chair for your friend, let her know about the amount of work involved, such as buying the wood, designing the chair, building it, and polishing it. This way, your friend will understand the steps involved and adjust her expectations accordingly.

I ordered a cell phone screen protector recently. In my mind, it was a simple screen protector and would not have taken effort to deliver through mail. To my surprise, it took three and a half weeks to arrive. Obviously there were complications in delivering it, but nobody in that company took the time to explain it to me. I was waiting for it to be delivered within a week and was about to cancel the credit card transaction when I received the package. If the vendor had managed expectations, I would have better understood the challenges they had in shipping this product to me.

Understanding expectation: While it is important to make a reasonable commitment, before we do, we need to understand what is expected of us. There are many factors relating to expectation.

First, we need to understand the deliverable; most of the time we have a quantifiable expectation that we can understand. For example, your friend might expect you to deliver 10 boxes of the product to him. Yet there are times when the expectation cannot be quantified. In those cases, try to quantify it on behalf of the other person. Salespeople are very good at this. For example, if you go to an investment adviser and say, "I want to have a happy retirement," the adviser might help you translate this into a monthly income.

Once we can quantify the expectation, we can then go on to understand what feelings are associated with this expectation. Would the deliverable that you provide make the person thrilled, happy, or merely satisfied? This way, you can associate how much the person's feelings are attached to your deliverable. You can adjust your commitment based on how they feel about it.

It is also important to understand what they define as exceeding expectation. Some of this would be implied, yet it is important to know it. For example, let's say you're the investment adviser and you can deliver $1,100 a month, which is clearly exceeding expectations by your standards. But, if the client defines exceeding expectations as $1,500, then your efforts won't be properly rewarded.

Same goes for not meeting expectations. In the previous example, you might deliver $950 and call it "not meeting expectations," but if the person was okay with having at least $900, you actually met their expectations. By understanding what the person defines as the failure point, you can more effectively manage your own expectations.

You will know also what is critical to achieve. Though the end deliverable might have a number of factors, only the critical factors in our mind determine the success of it.

Follow-up and feedback: A lot of marketing literature talks about managing expectations. I have yet to find something that talks comprehensively about providing status updates and feedback about the progress. A lot of our commitments and credibility depend on providing updates on where we are on things. As much as it is important to manage expectations, it is equally important keep your partners happy through letting them know how things are going. Providing status updates can be beneficial in a couple of ways:

▪ Providing updates on where things are with the deliverable keeps your contacts informed and comfortable. They would know what to expect and how things are going.

▪ Providing updates also gives you the opportunity to change the expectations if there are any problems with your deliverable. For example, if there is a delay in the project, you will be able to mention it in your updates rather than waiting until the last moment to let your contact know. Your network would consider you a reliable person who would keep them informed if something went wrong.

Providing feedback is particularly important when you are working on large projects. Most managers want to know where things stand. Some organizations have frequent structured processes to provide feedback to the management, but sometimes structured processes do not provide all the information required, so some informal update might be required.

Delivering results: Once you are ready to deliver on your commitment, it is important to connect your deliverable to what you originally promised. You do that by reminding the other person about the commitment you originally made. Any changes to the original commitment and why the changes were made can then be discussed. The reason this is important is because you are reminding the other person that you actively worked on the commitment you made. This reinforces your credibility as a person who delivers on his or her commitments.

Conclusion

Try to be service-oriented all the time. Try to help people whenever you can in whatever capacity you can. The more you make others feel important, the more they will carry you toward success. Success comes through people, and you need to win their trust and respect to be successful. Being service-oriented is one of the best ways to do that.

CHAPTER 15

TIME MANAGEMENT

Time management is a broad topic, yet it is another important aspect to be mastered for success. If you go to any bookstore, you will find several books on time management. This chapter is not intended to be all-encompassing, but it covers the most important aspects of time management.

 Time management is about getting the most value from the same 24 hours that everyone has.

Without a doubt, time management is very important. We all get the same 24 hours a day. Successful people achieve a great deal while ordinary people live life without much success. This difference has always made me curious as to what successful people do to make themselves successful. Having done research on many different aspects of time management, I have come to realize that there is no one answer. Many factors affect success, but time management plays a large role.

Principles of Time Management

Let's start with what time management is *not* about. I've seen many ordinary people going about their day-to-day activities. They have children's things to worry about, family activities, grocery shopping, and work. We are all busy. We run around getting these things done, and we feel good that our day is filled with things to do. Some people are happy that they are busy.

In the midst of all this chaos, we rarely have time to think. I agree it is a very fulfilling feeling to be useful throughout the day, but are we achieving what we really want to do in life? At some point in our lives, we will ask ourselves, "Is this all there is to life?" Before you can say that you have done something with your life, you need to achieve your purpose, and no one's purpose is to be busy for no reason. Unfortunately, most of us are just busy for no reason. At the end of the day, we haven't achieved much. We have just survived.

Time management is not about managing your busy schedule. It is about achieving your purpose so that you can satisfactorily say, "I have done something with my life" when the question comes to you.

On a day-to-day basis, we are busy doing our things. However, we rarely realize that the good things can keep you away from your best. We know good from bad, and we wouldn't get involved if our efforts weren't for a good cause. But to be successful, we must pare down some of the good activities and focus mostly on our best.

For example, at work, if you are managing your e-mail Inbox diligently and don't have time to take on projects that make a difference to the company, you will be viewed as just another worker. In order to get your next promotion, you need to make a difference. If you don't make the time to do your value-added projects, you will not be viewed as a person who can make a difference. Something needs to come off your plate in order for you to make this difference. This is what time management is all about. Time management is making sure you take your purpose and execute on it. It is not about managing your workload.

 Tools can't manage time for you. You need to manage your time using the tools. You are the master, not the slave.

Another thing to remember is that time management is not about tools and techniques. Tools and the techniques are merely there to help you. Most of us get sold on the next available phone or calendar managing our time. No, the tool will be yet another tool. The only thing that can manage your time is you. For that, you need to have the correct tools at your fingertips. I have gone through this process myself. The tools that I talk about in this chapter will help you, but they won't make you successful unless you start controlling yourself.

Time management is about being both efficient and effective.

Time management is not just about being efficient. It is about being both efficient and effective. The time that you spend needs to be connected to your purpose and strategy. Of course, you cannot avoid the everyday things that life throws at you. We all need to take care of the groceries, clean our houses, and do our laundry. It is how we achieve our purpose on top of the everyday tasks that makes us successful. Successful people also have everyday things to do. Yet they achieve their success over and above those.

Time management comes from within rather than without. What I mean by this is that you have to have the correct principles within you first: principles such as courage, control, purpose, and focus. Once you have the principles in place, then you can use tools such as calendars and to-do lists effectively.

Time management is a set of tools to

- Remind you what is important
- Identify the next steps
- Determine what needs to be done
- Schedule a time to do it

We not only get efficient but also effective. While efficiency is getting more done with your skills and abilities, being effective is all about doing the right things with your time. Your skills and abilities should be used to achieve your purpose in your life rather than merely keep you busy.

Focus

To get things done, we have to be focused and avoid distractions. This is a key principle of managing your time.

We can plan our time and schedule activities. However, if we don't focus, we'll get distracted and not make much progress on our priorities. In the environment that we live in, we have a lot of distractions.

For example, if we sit at our desk, the Internet and e-mail are there to distract us, and at home, there's always the TV to distract. It could even be something that is important, such as doing a quick cleanup in our house.

In fact, most of the things that we need to do to achieve our purpose are not as interesting as the things that distract us. This is why we have difficulty focusing. There will always be something that is more interesting than what we are doing. It is very easy to get distracted by directing our attention toward the more interesting things. Focusing on what needs to be done is difficult.

I have always struggled with focus. I noticed that I have a problem when I was in university. I was trying to get a project completed and I had to sit down and focus on doing the project. I spent more time trying to sit down and start the task than actually doing it. Then I started to research time management. As a result, I was better able to prioritize, schedule, and plan activities, yet I struggled for years not being able to execute most of the things that I planned. I would have all the tools that I needed to effectively manage my time, but I just could not execute. I was getting distracted with all the things around me. Sometimes, I even got distracted with the time-management tools themselves. I started to observe myself on what worked. The time-management techniques worked sometimes but not all the time. One thing I noticed was that once I had started a task, I could go on without a problem. It was starting that gave me a problem.

Finally one thing that worked was self-talk. When I tell myself that I need to focus, miraculously, I have little problem focusing myself and starting the tasks. We tend listen to ourselves far better than anyone else. Once I started to focus, I became tremendously productive. I was able to achieve things during a short period that I'd been struggling with for years.

Successful people go through the pain of doing difficult things that most of us don't want to do.

Being able to focus on what you have to do gives you tremendous productivity. To do the things that will move us closer to our ideal state is difficult. Sometimes, these activities are not interesting; they are mundane or downright painful. However, we have to cross the chasm and get them done. Successful people are the ones who are able to go through pain to do difficult things. This is what makes them successful. They are willing to do what most of us are not willing to do. It is human nature not to do the things that we don't like to do. Success comes to the few who can go that distance.

In order to do the things that we don't like to do, we have to focus ourselves on the tasks that will make us successful. Most of the time these tasks are painful and unpleasant, but do whatever it takes to make yourself focus on the important tasks. For me, it was self-talk. When I tell myself, "I will do this," I find it easy to focus. We are all different in our own ways, but one thing that is common to our success is that we need to focus our energy into one thing to be successful.

Prioritizing

 Your priorities should drive how you use your time.

Time management starts with prioritizing what you need to achieve. You cannot get everything done that you would like. It's a fact of life that we have to let go of some things in order to achieve important things. We all have only a limited amount of time in our lives. If we are to make our lives and our careers more productive and achieve success, we have to make choices. The priorities that we put against our tasks are our choices, and they need to align with our purpose during each phase.

I won't discuss specific techniques here, but no matter what techniques you use, time management boils down to achieving the most in your life within the span that we have—essentially achieving our mission.

In order to prioritize your life, the first step is to list all the activities you have to do. Go find a quiet place where you can brainstorm. Don't be judgmental or think about how and when to do it. Just list. Initially, a lot of to-dos on your mind will come up. It will slow down after you have listed most of the things you have to do. Try to remember as much as possible. You won't be able to list everything because some inevitably won't come to mind. It's okay not to have everything written down.

Once you complete this exercise, you'll likely feel a sense of relief. We keep a lot in our minds. When we decide to do something, it weighs on our minds for a long time, even though we don't always realize it. Now you are ready to move on to the next step: prioritizing these activities. You might have listed everything from work projects to simple tasks such as grocery shopping.

Let's start by marking the activities that are high priority. I know you probably would like to further prioritize and come up with a detailed action plan. While this is a great idea, when you overcomplicate your system, it becomes too cumbersome to manage in the long run. The system you have should be simple to manage and effective. If you have a complicated organization system, you will resent using this system.

> You need to have a set of criteria that will help you to prioritize your activities.

The priorities should be given according to criteria that work for you. The following illustration is an example of a prioritization scheme. Of course, this is what worked for me. What would work for you might be different. So you need to have your own set of priorities. The priorities that worked for me are as follows:

Priority A: These are activities that are directly connected to my purpose and mission. Many of these activities are not urgent. If I don't actively plan for these, they would most likely not move at all. They are important in achieving my purpose, but they can wait. For example, writing a book is not something that will break my bank account. Therefore, there is no urgency for me. However, if I don't do it, I would be wasting my life. These activities are immensely important activities for me. There is no external force or deadline pushing me to get these activities done. They depend solely on my discipline to get done. If I don't have the discipline and I don't push myself, these activities will not go anywhere. Furthermore, these activities are not pleasant to do.

Priority B: These activities are important, and if I don't get them done, I will have to face some consequences. This bucket might have work-related activities that my boss expects me to get done. If I don't, I could lose my job or miss out on a promotion. Also, these could be time-sensitive. For example, if you are doing an exam that needs to be completed by the end of the year and that would affect your career progress, it would fall under this category. You don't have to push yourself to get these activities done because there will be an external force that is pushing you to get this done. These activities might or might not be pleasant, but you are compelled to get them done.

Priority C: These are the maintenance activities that need to be done in order to support the two previous priorities. If you don't get these activities done or delay them too long, your ability to execute on the two previous priorities would be affected. There will be an external force pushing you to get these done, such as a deadline. But these activities are not directly connected with your mission and purpose. These include activities such as attending to your physical health, paying your bills on time, and having a sound financial base. These activities are important support activities for your mission. They would be bugging you on an ongoing basis. You have to attend to these activities, and some of these activities are not pleasant to do.

Priority D: These are pleasant activities, and you would not have any problem getting yourself to do these activities. However, they are not at all connected with the mission or do not support it. Examples of these activities are things like watching TV, reading a light novel, going to the movies, and keeping up with gossip. We all need to do these at some point or another. However, they are not essential. Not doing these activities will not affect your success.

Similarly, you need to come up with your own set of priorities that will suit your career and your lifestyle. You might not view life and career the same way I do. Some of these priorities might not be suitable for you. You need to build your own priority system that will work for you. These priorities are buckets to organize your time.

Once you have decided on your priorities, you need to go back to your list of tasks and categorize each task according to priority. You will then have a system for planning them.

For example, I need to plan for my Priority A tasks first thing in the morning. I am prone to distraction while I am doing them, and putting them off will keep me away from achieving my mission. Priority

B tasks are what I do during the day because I have to. I don't have to push myself to get them done. I have every Friday night to complete my Priority C tasks such as paying my bills, cleaning my filing system, and sorting things that were piling up during the week. Priority D tasks are kept for when I have some time such as Saturday night, when I have some time to relax.

Depending on your level of energy and your style of doing things, you can come up with a way to categorize your tasks. In the next section, we will discuss how to manage your time based on your priorities. However, keep in mind that I will be using my prioritization scheme to illustrate how to do it.

Managing Your Time

Once you prioritize your activities, you can then start managing your time and executing your activities. They should be executed by the priority you classified. There are two types of activities:

1. **Time-sensitive activities:** We can give a specific time to achieve these activities. In order to plan for these activities, we need a calendaring tool. There are many calendaring tools available. They could be as advanced as computerized calendaring tools or as manual as a paper organizer—whichever you feel comfortable using.

2. **Non-time-sensitive activities:** We would not have a specific time to achieve these activities. This is essentially a task list. Most calendaring tools come with a task list that can be used to organize these types of activities. These are the activities that have one or more of the following characteristics:
   - They are waiting to be scheduled in a calendar and are parked in your task list as a reminder.
   - They cannot have a specific time slot but need to be done at the earliest opportunity.
   - Parked to be planned later.

You can schedule your activities based on your priority and the type of activity in your system.

It's human nature to put off Priority A activities because there is no direct incentive to do them. Hence some of our most important activities get pushed to the side.

The highest priority items should be planned, scheduled, and acted on before you do anything.

In your time-management plan, you should be planning on doing your Priority A activities first. They are the ones which will have the greatest impact on your success. They should be scheduled and planned as meetings with you and executed diligently. Because they don't have a specific time to be completed, you have to manually set aside time to complete them. Once you decide the time, then you can use your calendaring tool to schedule these activities. You set a specific time with yourself to work on these activities.

Our most important activities are procrastinated most of the time because we fear these activities. There are many types of fears. We could fear that we won't be able to do a great job with the task and hence put it off. Or we fear that we would not be able to figure out a solution to the task or we fear confronting someone and asking for a favor. You need to overcome these fears and move forward despite your fears. We cannot do a perfect job in our first take on a task. If we need to speak to someone to get our task done, we have to speak to that person; hiding will not get us anywhere. We have to make the time in our schedules to execute our Priority A activities.

Once they're scheduled, we have to overcome our fears and focus on getting the Priority A activities completed as planned in our calendaring tool. It would be pointless if you scheduled these activities and let other Priority B, C, and D activities take over the time of Priority A activities. Because there is no one watching over you to get you to complete these activities, you have to monitor yourself and get these done. Focus is very important in getting these done. You have to be your own master and tell yourself to do these activities.

Sometimes, the activities you would have are projects, which means that you would have other smaller activities that make up the project. For example, if your Priority A activity were to complete an exam to get your certification, first you would have to plan what activities need to be done; only once you had that planned could you go about doing the individual activities. You would use the Strategic Planning Framework discussed in Chapter 5, "Strategizing Your Career and

Life," to plan for these activities. Planning the activity would be your first step and first activity.

Once you schedule your Priority A activities, then you can go and start scheduling your Priority B and C activities in that order. Of course, most Priority B and C activities would have specific deadlines attached to them. You would give yourself ample time to get these activities done and schedule them. Even if you don't have a specific time to do them, it's always good to set aside some specific time. When you have a meeting with yourself, you have a psychological reason to do it and a specific time to get the work done. If for some reason the time that you scheduled is not enough, before the activity is finished, you could schedule the next time to get it done.

Some of Priority B and C activities, such as paying bills, could be small enough that you might want to group them into one timeframe. For example, you could have all your Priority C activities done on Friday between 7 and 8 PM. Similarly, you could review your work e-mails every morning from 9 to 10. This way, you would have time to get these done.

Priority D activities would be anytime in between Priority A, B, and C activities. Because you would not have any problem starting these activities, you could do them anytime. You would have the motivation to do these anytime you like. Even if these activities were procrastinated, it would not affect your destiny.

Similarly, you need to have a method to execute your activities. You need to use your tools to organize yourself. In order to succeed, you have to be organized. Most people who are organized automatically become successful.

Conclusion

Time management is crucial to your success. Time management essentially means organizing yourself to achieve your highest priorities. Successful people achieve a lot in their lives. They use time management to prioritize and execute the things they need to do most in order to get the greatest value from their time. We all have the same 24 hours. It is up to us to make the most of them.

CHAPTER 16

ACKNOWLEDGING
ACCOMPLISHMENTS

You are a great person. You are great because of the things you have achieved, no matter how big or small they are. At every turning point in your life, you have made decisions, and accomplished things that have made you who you are right now. Though you might not realize it, these are great things. They are your achievements. If you didn't do what you needed to do, you would have ended up being a very different person than you are right now.

We need to frequently recognize our accomplishments.

Do you recognize this greatness in you frequently? If not, don't feel bad. Very few of us do. It is important to recognize this greatness in yourself because it brings self-confidence to be successful.

You look at your physical appearance in the mirror frequently, but do you look at your personality frequently in the same way? You should look at yourself frequently to know how great you have been. Looking at your personality has many advantages. Recognizing your accomplishments will take you even further by giving you a great sense of confidence. At the same time, it will show you what has worked in your life and help you to be even more effective in your life ahead.

Wherever you want to go in life, it is very important to know where you came from and what you did to get to where you are right now. You don't have to be a great leader to have accomplishments.

However great or small your achievements and accomplishments, they are still your achievements.

My wife is a great person, even though she does not have her name published anywhere. She had almost no childhood when she was growing up due to numerous family problems. However, she ended up getting married and leaving her past behind to have a wonderful family today. The little decisions she made and the choices she made are her accomplishments. She is a great person today because of those little accomplishments. If she hadn't done what she did, she could have been completely lost. She walks tall today because of those accomplishments.

Keeping Track of Accomplishments

It is important to keep track of these accomplishments and the things you have done. It is easy for us to think about the things that we have not done. Most of us look at things that we have not done in our life. This is our nature as humans. However, you need to keep track of the good things that you have done. This is the most important thing to do. When you look back at the good things that you have done, even the smallest things, you start to gain confidence in yourself and start to appreciate the greatness within you. This is why it is important to track your progress. By looking back, you gain sense of the enormous achievement.

It is easy to keep track of your accomplishments. Pick a quiet time. It is going to be a time for self-reflection. Try to recall the important moments in your life, just like watching a movie. On a paper or on your computer, make a list of good things you have done. Don't judge these accomplishments, just brainstorm them. Sometimes it is best to do this alone. It does not have to be complete. When you feel you have put most of your accomplishments down, take a look at this list. Add up each positive addition and look at the total picture. This list should show you how great you've been and what has worked in your life. Maintain this list by frequently adding to it and reviewing it often.

    Every small achievement is an achievement.

Even the largest monuments are built by combining the smallest grains of sand. Each grain is put together to form a brick, and each brick is put together to form a monument. This is what you are today—a great monument. Whoever you are, every little thing that you have done and the choices you have made, have affected you both positively and negatively. You might have gone through a bad divorce; even though it resulted in heartache, it also made you a stronger person. Take a look at of all the positive things in each situation that has made you who you are today.

We don't generally realize how ordinary things that we have achieved in the course of our lives affect us. Simple things make such a big difference in our lives. I remember an e-mail that I replied to that played such a pivotal role in the level of confidence I have about my job. For an ordinary person, it would have been one of the thousands of e-mail replies they have written. In this e-mail, I defended a position that only I believed in. It was right after I started my career and in an environment full of experienced people, it was tough to stand on my own. My opinion was accepted by others in the end. For me, it was an indication that I knew my job well and that I was confident of my profession. In my list of accomplishments, I wrote this incident down. When I look back at it, I see that I was great at that moment. Should I have forgotten it and let it be one of my thousand e-mail replies, then the greatness in that moment would have been lost. This goes to show that as humans, we need to be reminded how great we are. We get caught up in the spur of the moment, and we don't realize how wonderful we have been even in the smallest moment.

Looking back at your strengths is similar to looking at yourself in a sudden, unexpected reflection. Have you had those moments when you unexpectedly see your reflection? There is an image that you carry in your mind about you, and when you see yourself in that reflection, it startles you. You become self-aware. This is because the image in your mind is different from your actual image. Even though you have seen yourself a thousand times before, it catches you by surprise. It feels as if you suddenly woke up. Looking at your accomplishments is very similar. You realize how strong and great you have been. You'd be surprised at the outcome.

Knowing What Works for You

 Looking at your accomplishments will reveal your strengths and weaknesses.

If you don't look at yourself and what you have achieved, it will be very difficult for you to know what is working and what isn't in your life. To be effective, you need to know what works in your life and what you are good at. When you look at your accomplishments, you will know what you are good at and what works. You can capitalize on these strengths to be successful.

I have always thought I was good at mathematics and accounting. Looking back at my accomplishments, I realize writing works in my life more than mathematics. It is something that I really enjoy doing. This has been a subtle message through my accomplishments. And I wouldn't have realized it if I didn't look back at my achievements.

Conclusion

It is important to look at your accomplishments. Just as you look at yourself in the mirror to view your physical appearance, you need to look at your accomplishments to see who you really are. You need to list your accomplishments at each turning point in your life and look at it. It gives the view of yourself that you have been missing. Looking back at what you have achieved will tell you what works for you in your life. Most important, it shows how great you've been throughout the years. It doesn't matter who you are in your life. You are great. You just need to realize it and recognize it.

CHAPTER 17

LIVING YOUR DREAMS AND MAKING IT HAPPEN

 Dreams inspire us and drive us to be great.

We are blessed because we can dream. Dreams guide us to be great. They give us the energy to fly. All the achievements in humanity have happened because we are able to dream. Without dreams, there wouldn't be any imagination or creativity. Without dreams, we wouldn't be human. Having dreams makes us feel alive and motivated. We are able to imagine and create in our minds before a single ounce of effort has been put into work. It is dreaming that has made us who we are today and will continue to take us to the future. What a great ability we have!

Yet we often downplay dreaming. We forget that it is our dreams that have brought humanity to its modern existence. The world advances because of dreams. If all our ideas were practical and realistic, they would never advance mankind. We would always be thinking within our known boundaries.

As children, we dreamed a lot. These dreams drive us to become mature adults. As we grow up, most of us lose touch with our ability to dream. Reality sets in to our worlds, and the difficulty of life starts to surface. We start to think that dreaming doesn't yield anything in life. We stop fighting for our dreams and write them off as child's play.

Yet the few who retain their ability to dream are considered visionaries. They have great achievements and win the admiration of the world.

We all need to dream all over again. It is alright to dream. The difference now is that you need to work at your dreams. You need to put effort into making your dreams reality. Dreaming gives us the energy to achieve. Once you have a dream, putting in the effort and working hard are second nature; work is no longer *work*.

We all need to get back to dreaming. We need to put effort into achieving our dreams. Life is difficult. For us to think that life should be handed to us on a platter without problems or obstacles is a fallacy. "Happily ever after" doesn't exist. Achieving your dreams is even more difficult.

Dreams are difficult to hold on to. They wouldn't be dreams if they were easy. People around you might not understand your dreams. Most of them might not even approve of your dreams. But you need to hold on to them because they are your dreams. Dreams might not sound practical. That is why people often do not understand them, even their own. People who make their dreams a reality do it through this difficulty. We give up our dreams because it is difficult when we should be holding on to them.

Life is a privilege. For us to make this life great, we have to put effort into it. To make an effort and go beyond our commitments is a choice that we all need to make. It is our choice either to achieve our dreams or to give them up, so make the choice to live your dreams.

Never give up your dreams. Successful people make their dreams happen.

Dreams don't come to you; you make your own dreams. You start creating the world you want in your mind. This is what dreaming is all about. You then go on to build your dream one piece at a time. To achieve a dream might seem like a big task, which is why we all think dreaming is child's play. However, people who have achieved their dreams also started one piece at a time.

Here's my dream: I want to build a successful accounting practice someday. I dream of having my own large office with successful accountants working for me. I go in the morning through the glass door to my company. There is a wonderful reception area with leather chairs. There are offices where well-dressed professionals work. I go to my office passing these offices. I start my day trying to help other companies do well by managing their money.

Without a penny to invest, this is just a fantasy. But I have a small printer that I can use to print brochures, so I will design and print a brochure today. Tomorrow, after I come back from work, I will go and distribute it to 10 small businesses. I will walk door to door and find my first client. This is what working on your dreams is all about. I believe in this dream, and I will chip away one piece at a time. Always take steps as long as they are in the direction of your dream. You will get there someday. Don't stand still thinking that your dreams are too big to achieve. You'd be surprised by how they come true when you chip away at them.

Reality kills our dreams. We live in a world where dreams are viewed as a fantasy. This is because the modern world is all about what you can see and feel. Very few of us realize that it is dreams that built this world. People who have achieved great things, built large corporations, and invented great things are actually dreamers. They dreamed first and then achieved their dream. Most of us don't want to put in the effort required to achieve our dreams; when we fail in the first attempt, we begin thinking dreams are just fantasies. We tell our children and people around us self-fulfilling excuses about our dreams. Yet people who are successful are the people who hold on to their dreams and put effort into doing what it takes to achieve them.

When urgency calls, we often give up our non-urgent commitments to do the task. Most of the time, these are our dreams. Most of us give our dreams a low priority and give up ourselves for others. As we get older, we regret not having lived our lives to the fullest and not achieving our dreams. We lose sight of what is important. It is the good that keeps us from our best. So put yourself first. Make your dreams your first priority.

Dreaming gives us tremendous energy. It inspires us and guides us to be better than who we are. Remember when you were a child, the inspiration you had when someone asked you what you wanted to be when you grew up? Every child's eyes brighten up when you ask them what they want to be when they grow up. This is the power of dreams. They have a tremendous power to inspire you and give you energy to move forward. Never lose sight of your dreams.

When you have a dream and hold on to your dream, something strange happens. Somehow nature brings all its efforts together to make your dream come true. My conclusion is that nature provides opportunities only based on need. When you hold on to your dreams, you send the message to nature communicating your need. The book *The Secret* is all about this concept. I have personally experienced the power of dreams, and I have spoken to so many people who have experienced the same. When you hold on to your dreams, it is as if you are telling nature how badly you want your dreams to come true. Nature then rearranges opportunities around you to make them come true. Most who hold on to their dreams long enough know that the dreams do come true. Hold on to it no matter how difficult it is, and work on it one step at a time. Somehow the universe transcends to deliver to you the dreams that you want.

Dreams give us wings to fly.

Conclusion

I know all of this sounds like it is from a fairy tale, but dreams really give us the energy to reach our best. We often downplay our dreams. Dreams are what drive you to your goals. The people that do not pursue their dreams are the ones who get stuck with ordinary day-to-day life. You need to hold on to your dreams and make them happen. Never give them up, no matter how big they are or how unachievable they may seem. Dreaming is the most amazing thing in this world. It gives you energy and it rejuvenates you. Believe in your dreams and make an effort to make them come true. They are your dreams. It is all you have. Protect them. Make them come true.

INDEX

COURSE TECHNOLOGY
CENGAGE Learning™

Professional • Technical • Referen…

COURSE TECHNOLOGY PTR has numerous books that will help you maximize the job search process or excel in your current career. From creating the perfect résumé and acing the interview to developing the overall on-the-job skill set, we provide a comprehensive library of tools that will help you land the job of your dreams and work your way up the corporate ladder once you've got it.

90 DAYS TO SUCCESS SERIES

The first three months on the job are the most important! For those who have already landed the job and are eager to hit the ground running from Day 1, we provide the *90 Days to Success* series. These books provide expert advice and action plans for achievement from executives who have been in your shoes before and want to share their considerable experience.

90 DAYS TO SUCCESS AS A MANAGER

1-59863-865-3 • $19.99 • 232 PGS

90 DAYS TO SUCCESS AS A PROJECT MANAGER

1-59863-869-6 • $19.99 • 376 PGS

90 DAYS TO SUCCESS IN FUNDRAISING

1-59863-876-9 • $19.99 • 272 PGS

90 DAYS TO SUCCESS IN CONSULTING

1-4354-5442-1 • $19.99 • 336 PGS

90 DAYS TO SUCCESS IN GRANT WRITING

1-4354-5486-3 • $19.99 • 272 PGS

101 SERIES

Create the perfect résumé. Ace the interview. Hone your skills. Books in the *101* series provide complete "get the job" advice from career experts for anyone seeking new employment. Tips are presented in an easy-to-read, pithy format, and each book is only $12.99 so getting the new job doesn't have to break the bank!

101 GREAT RÉSUMÉS
THIRD EDITION

1-59863-855-6 • $12.99 • 216 PGS

101 WAYS TO MAKE YOURSELF INDISPENSABLE AT WORK

1-4354-5432-4 • $12.99 • 208 PGS

101 SMART QUESTIONS TO ASK ON YOUR INTERVIEW
THIRD EDITION

1-59863-854-8 • $12.99 • 168 PGS

101 GREAT ANSWERS TO THE TOUGHEST INTERVIEW QUESTIONS
SIXTH EDITION

1-59863-853-X • $12.99 • 200 PGS

PERSPECTIVES™ SERIES

Ever wonder what your clients, customers, or employees *really* think of the job you're doing? Find out with the *Perspectives*™ series. In *Perspectives*, two or more successful executives share their opinions, but never collaborate, ensuring unbiased and unfiltered views of business topics such as increasing sales, building brands, marketing tactics, and managing employees. The frank "he said/she said" format of these books provides a unique learning experience as well as an entertaining read!

PERSPECTIVES ON INCREASING SALES

1-59863-874-2 • $29.99 • 311 PGS

PERSPECTIVES ON BRANDING

1-59863-872-6 • $29.99 • 276 PGS

PERSPECTIVES ON MANAGING EMPLOYEES

1-59863-873-4 • $29.99 • 300 PGS

PERSPECTIVES ON MARKETING

1-59863-871-8 • $29.99 • 377 PGS

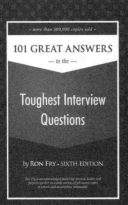
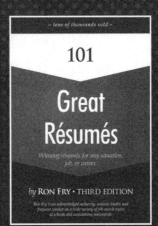